22 MINUTES

22 MINUTES

The USS Vincennes *and the Tragedy of Savo Island*
A Lifetime Survival Story

Jeff Spevak

LYONS PRESS
Guilford, Connecticut

An imprint of The Rowman & Littlefield Publishing Group, Inc.
Distributed by NATIONAL BOOK NETWORK

British Library Cataloguing in Publication Information Available

Library of Congress Cataloging-in-Publication Data

Name: Spevak, Jeff, author.
Title: 22 minutes : the USS Vincennes and the tragedy of Savo Island : a lifetime survival story / Jeff
    Spevak.
Other titles: Twenty two minutes
Description: Lanham, MD : Lyons Press, An Imprint of The Rowman & Littlefield Publishing
    Group, Inc., [2019] | Includes bibliographical references and index.
Identifiers: LCCN 2018052115 (print) | LCCN 2018054544 (ebook) | ISBN 9781493038282 (elec-
    tronic) | ISBN 9781493038275 (cloth : alk. paper)
Subjects: LCSH: Coleman, Ernie. | Savo Island, Battle of, Solomon Islands, 1942. | Vincennes
    (Cruiser : CA-44) | World War, 1939–1945—Personal narratives, American.
Classification: LCC D774.S318 (ebook) | LCC D774.S318 S64 2019 (print) | DDC 940.54/26593092
    [B]—dc23
LC record available at https://lccn.loc.gov/2018052115

Printed in the United States of America

"Sailing is my life."

ONE

It is ninety-one steps to the top of El Castillo, amid the ancient ruins of Chichen Itza. Add up the steps on each of the four sides, plus the platform at the top, and it comes to 365. One step for each day in a year of anyone's life. As both the steps and the years add up, the climb gets more difficult. "I got to the top and—foof!—I collapsed," the old guy says. Fellow tourists rushed up to him. "Are you all right?"

"'Leave me alone,' he told them. 'I just need to lie here for a few minutes.'"

He did not believe that he might die there, at the top of a Mayan pyramid. Never considered that it could happen—although perhaps such a climb in the Mexican sun was not the wisest expenditure of time for a man who was then eighty-two years old. A man out of his element—water. Ernie Coleman sailed, an amateur racer who filled his home with decades of trophies. His boat wasn't always the fastest on Lake Ontario, but Ernie knew the tricks that could ease his craft over the finish line first, especially on days when the wind was elusive.

When I first met Ernie, he was sitting at a patio table beneath an enormous tulip tree. I sat in the chair on the other side of the table and studied the guy, my subject for the next few months, while he studied me, his biographer. Ernie was ninety-three and looked a little battered, but he moved about easily enough thanks to some rewiring and a few replacement parts he'd acquired over the last decade. His mind seemed crisp as I prodded him for the details of his life. A man who had been caught up amid life's largest moments, a child of the Great Depression, a graduate of the Greatest Generation. A carpenter, Ernie built things, and he rebuilt his life repeatedly, struggling through divorce and the deaths of two wives. With the marriages came one adopted child and seven stepkids. He adapted to change. He was a survivor.

A large part of the appeal of a guy like Ernie is that so many of us know a man or woman like him—a grandfather, a distant aunt—though we don't know their stories. Some of their experiences serve as modest life lessons. Others are remarkable adventures. In a metaphor to which any sailor can relate, each episode of Ernie's life can be thought of as a thread. When gathered up and wound together, the threads create a strong rope—a rope he unconsciously relied on in times of crisis. The more threads, the stronger the rope, the stronger the character.

The navy had taken Ernie to see the world, first during World War II, then the Korean War. He didn't always like what he'd seen. Maui? "It was so perfect, it was monotonous." And he refused to think of the Solomon Islands. Ernie was a short man, even before losing a few inches to age, but broad shouldered, with the large, knotted hands of his builder's trade. When I first brought up the Battle of Savo Island, he waved his hands in front of him for a moment, as though pushing away the memory. It was not a story he shared, even though he lived in the shadow of that experience.

"I know why those kids come back from Afghanistan and shoot themselves," he said sadly one morning, sitting on the shady patio at his home.

"You lay awake at night, reacting, reacting, reacting. Because it's so real."

His was a lifetime spent with one purpose in mind: to sail away, to exchange the nightmares for beautiful evenings sailing off the coast of Lake Ontario.

In his eighth decade, at an age when most men had settled down in front of the television to wait for the end, Ernie was still sailing. But the waters were increasingly uncharted. He'd climbed those ninety-one steps that day in 1998 because he was trying to impress the woman he was courting—Marilyn, twenty-five years his junior.

"This guy's really elderly," she remembers thinking when she first met him. She'd placed an ad in the personals section of the newspaper, seeking a man who liked sailing and travel. She checked out twenty-seven respondents. Nothing. He was the twenty-eighth.

Marilyn was a travel agent who was showing him the world, watching to see if Ernie could keep up. He could. He went to Rome with her several times, examining ancient aqueducts with his builder's eye. He sailed the Caribbean on a five-masted clipper ship. "Four hundred feet long," Marilyn says. "Four hundred and thirty-nine feet," Ernie corrects. The captain had even let him take the wheel for a while, as tourists took pictures of Ernie. A real curiosity, they must have thought, like one of those water-skiing squirrels.

Marilyn took him snow skiing for the first time when he was eighty. "After six lessons, I was skiing with her," Ernie insists. "In fact, I was holding back."

"No, you weren't," Marilyn chides him.

"You're a pleasure skier," Ernie says. He was a competitor. He chased Marilyn, and he caught her. Now they were married, living in the Madison Terrace house Ernie rebuilt just a couple of hundred yards from Lake Ontario Beach. A house with a small window facing north. He looked out that window every morning to see what was happening on Lake Ontario. The view changed every day.

But first, he had to get off that Mexican pyramid. His fellow tourists were worried that the old man was dying at Chichen Itza, even as he marveled at how, while standing at one pyramid in the ruined complex, "you holler and get seven echoes." And at "the sacrificial pool, where they threw the maidens." And the precision of the architecture, functioning as a giant stone calendar, the sheer size of the project allowing him to dismiss the fact that "they were off a little."

Ernie was off a little himself. The shortness of breath? The first signs of congenital heart disease. A stent would later help take care of that. But there is only so much that modern medicine can do for a man.

"I caught my breath, and I was OK," Ernie says. Then he got up and walked down the pyramid.

TWO

Julie Lockner found me on the internet. She called from her home in Boston and asked if she could interest me in writing a book about her stepfather, Ernie Coleman. I'd be paid, of course. "He's a really cool old guy," she said. "He's ninety-three years old, lived through the Depression. He's been married four times."

Well, a lot of us have really cool old guys in the family. Doesn't make it a book. And quite frankly, I don't do sentimental.

"He's a sailing legend on Lake Ontario."

Better. But still not enough.

"He was in World War II. His ship was sunk in a battle." She didn't know the name of the ship, except that it started with the letter V, and the battle had been in the Pacific. "He doesn't like to talk about it."

Was it a freighter? A tanker? A warship?

"A big warship," she said.

I forget people's faces and where I left my car keys, but I have one of those brains that tucks away stuff like batting averages, song titles, and ship names. And I read a lot of history. There weren't a lot of big ships sunk during World War II with names that start with the letter V. In fact, when I looked it up a few moments after that conversation, I saw that there was only one, the one that I was vaguely recalling having been lost during the Battle of Savo Island: USS *Vincennes*.

What could be the overarching theme of the book quickly became apparent during that first telephone conversation: the eloquent silence and beauty of sailing on Lake Ontario contrasted with the horror of naval warfare—if Julie could correctly answer one question about her step-father: "He's ninety-three. Is he lucid?"

I will simply say that Ernie Coleman would make a fool of me.

* * *

Ernie, as it turned out, lived just a five-minute drive from my house. Julie insisted there was a story in this old man. After meeting him for the first time, I thought she might be right. Please don't call me an opportunist, a writer who preys on tragedy, death, drama—the tools of the trade. But when I saw for myself that Ernie had an unusually powerful memory for details and confirmed that he indeed had been on a ship that had been sunk in a major World War II battle in the South Pacific, I thought there might be a chance that I would write that book.

The Battle of Savo Island, the first of several naval battles during the Guadalcanal campaign, was the worst open-sea defeat in the history of the U.S. Navy. In twenty-two minutes, four big cruisers—three American, one Australian—were left burning and sinking. More than a thousand sailors lost their lives, including 332 on *Vincennes*. One-third of Ernie's shipmates died aboard *Vincennes* when it rolled over in the early morning darkness and descended to the muddy floor of Iron Bottom Sound, so named because it is the graveyard of so many ships and their crews.

* * *

I pull up to Ernie's house for our first meeting. It's low and pale green with the outline of a sailboat, cut from plywood, mounted high on the outside of a second-floor addition toward the back of the building. In the driveway are a couple of cars, including an old yellow van. I peer into its windows. The van is full of tools.

Ernie is sitting on the patio, waiting for me. We are an odd couple. He, forty years older than me, balding, a veteran. I—more than a foot taller and a newspaper rock critic with hair falling past my shoulders—never served in the military. But we hit it off immediately. There was common ground; more accurately, common water. Ernie was a sailor; I'd done some sailing. We had sailor friends and their boats in common. Fred Karshick and *Patriot*. Joel Roemer and *American Eagle*. Veterans who looked back on a few epic years in their lives when naming their boats. Roemer had been in the Battle of Peleliu, a vicious fight with the Japanese late in World War II over an island of negligible strategic value.

Ernie even had refinished the wood trim on *Eagle*. I'd crossed Lake Ontario on both of those boats and learned useful stuff like, if you're caught in a lightning storm while in the middle of the lake, don't hang on to the metal handrails.

Ernie reminded me of my father-in-law, who'd passed away a few years earlier. Similar build and demeanor, a familiar squareness of presence hiding an imp's character. I recognized the signs of clever, inventive men who played life with charm. Dick Rattray spent much of World War II as an Army Air Force mechanic in Iceland. Like Ernie, he didn't talk much about the war. Vets rarely do. My father-in-law told me a few anecdotes about wounded B-17 Flying Fortresses seeking refuge in Reykjavík, their fuselages riddled with bullet holes after combat in Europe. How difficult it was to work on the planes, with nuts and bolts snapping in the freezing temperatures. And how he and a buddy used hammers to flatten Icelandic coins and weave them into bracelets to sell to airmen passing through, so the guys would have something to take to their girls back home.

Ernie, I would discover, shared that kind of self-contained, entrepreneurial savvy.

We met virtually every Monday morning the summer and fall of 2010 at his home in Summerville, a lakeshore neighborhood in Rochester, New York, always under that big tulip tree unless it was raining. There were moments when Ernie struggled with a detail. But for the most part, the stories flowed. Ernie looked at life with a carpenter's eye: What makes it work? Who knew that you could use a shell casing from a five-inch naval gun to rig a muffler for a 1928 Dodge Victory Six?

Our first full session, following that get-acquainted meeting where I learned he'd survived the Mayan pyramid, began with an unfurling of local history as witnessed by Ernie, told with the relaxed pace of a beautiful sailboat outing. Here, Ernie's memory was most startling. He recalled many of those race details—the weather, his strategy, where he finished—with amazing clarity.

This would be a small, thoughtful book about a guy swept up in a century of big and little moments. With Ernie himself emerging as a compelling and remarkable character. A resourceful fellow who scrapped to survive in a fashion that seems quaint today. It's a mentality associated with his generation. A pride in self-reliance. He was a sailor who loved to dance and party, who needed to surround himself with people.

But always lurking behind the story was *Vincennes*.

Out of our conversations was born a book that Ernie's family self-published in the spring of 2012, *Chasing the Wind: The Humble, Epic Century of a Sailor*. The idea of chasing the wind is not simply how a sailor moves about on a lake; it is a metaphor for our pursuit of the elusive.

In Ernie's case, I think that was peace of mind.

THREE

The color of your hair and eyes, the shape of your ears, and perhaps how long you will live is encoded in the genes in your body in long strands of deoxyribonucleic acid. DNA. It is the basic blueprint of your life. Somewhere within the double helixes of Ernie Coleman's DNA, mixed among the genes for woodworking, were powerful genes for sailing. Genes that led him instinctively to water, complete with hardwiring for reading the wind, finding the good air.

Ernie begins his story with those genes. Handed down to him, he figures, by his grandparents. For many years, in the late 1800s and into the early part of the twentieth century, George and Clara Coleman owned a Thames sailing barge, a flat-bottomed boat designed to haul coal, mud, bricks, or grain along the Thames estuary. From what Ernie learned, George and Clara's boat, named *Hope*, was about seventy feet long, a little smaller than the norm for such a vessel, with a spritsail rigging that maximized maneuverability on the crowded Thames, while still strong enough to handle the ocean winds, allowing the couple to sail back and forth from London to Liverpool.

"It was rigged in such a way," Ernie says, "that when they came to a bridge, the mast folded down, they glided under, and cranked it back up."

It could not have been peaceful sailing, at least when loading or un-loading the boat. In *London: The Biography*, Peter Ackroyd describes the Thames riverside of that era as "filled with the sound of carts, horses, cranes and human voices, mingling with the whistles of the railway." He paints a picture of "factories and warehouses approaching as close to the water as they dared, while its wharves and mills and landing stages pulsated with the energies of human life and activities."

This crew of two—George and Clara, often accompanied by a paid hand—also apparently lived on the boat, an intimate arrangement that eventually produced two more crewmen, their sons, George and Albert. But the boys were not destined for life under the brownish-red sails of the Thames sailing barges. As they reached their twenties at the turn of the last century, they were sent away to America. George and Clara sold *Hope* and followed later.

"America was the opportunity," Ernie says. "Anyone who wanted to advance themselves came to America."

They were Ellis Island immigrants. The story Ernie tells is the same recited by millions of Americans—but not all Americans, of course. Not the ones who arrived from Africa in chains or the ones who survived the rapidly growing nation's genocidal wars against the native people who had been living there for centuries. Or the Mexican citizens who suddenly found themselves Californians and Texans when their country lost the Mexican-American War. Or the residents of South American countries in the twenty-first century who migrated north because their families in the United States told them, "Come here, it is better, and your government isn't trying to kill you."

American history casts a kinder light on the Ellis Island immigrants, although they certainly arrived with no guarantees. Ernie does not know why the family chose to send the boys to Rochester in western New York. He had heard, perhaps in eavesdropping on the conversations of adults when he was a child, that the city at the southern edge of Lake Ontario was chosen for the unlikely reason that there was a Rochester not far from London. That particular Rochester was, in fact, where many of the Thames sailing barges were constructed. Perhaps it was stamped or stenciled on one of the fittings on George and Clara's boat, a word they stared at for years while sailing, subliminally planted in their minds until the name became familiar.

Rochester.

Like London, Rochester was a boomtown bisected by a river with busy industry crowding its shores. Power plants, more than a dozen breweries, and mills powered by big wheels that turned in channels, called races, filled with water redirected from the river. Railroad tracks, including those bearing the coach cars of the Buffalo, Rochester, and Pittsburgh

Railways, curved gracefully down to the river's edge to meet the SS *Ontario No. 1*, a ferry that in five hours could carry one thousand passengers and railcars loaded with coal across the lake to Cobourg, the Canadian town fifty-two miles directly north. Unlike the Thames, however, the Genesee River was not crowded with freight-carrying boats, lake steamers, and barges or the pleasure craft of the Rochester Yacht Club—at least, not beyond two and a half miles where the river emptied into the lake. An imposing set of waterfalls saw to that.

Young George landed a job as a draftsman at Eastman Kodak, the Rochester company whose simplification of the photo process—making it a snap—had taken the camera out of the hands of professionals and turned every family outing into a postcard opportunity. He met another recent English immigrant, May. They married and soon had two children themselves: Frank and, four years later in 1916, Ernie.

Ernie did not remember his father. With the United States plunging into World War I, George never had the opportunity to be a part of what President Woodrow Wilson optimistically called "a war to end all wars." The influenza pandemic of 1918 killed an estimated 675,000 Americans, ten times as many U.S. citizens as would die in the war. Worldwide, perhaps twenty to forty million died of influenza. George Coleman was among them.

People who knew Ernie Coleman always said that he was an average guy who was caught up in some remarkable circumstances. Family circumstances early in his life certainly show as much. The math suggests that being two years old and fatherless was not an unusual situation. The life expectancy of a man born in the late 1880s in the United States, as was George Coleman, was forty-two and a half years. He made it to twenty-seven. Walk around the cemeteries where those of this generation now rest and it becomes quite obvious from the dates on the graves that, in dying young, George Coleman was pretty average. As was his brother, Albert, who died shortly thereafter of diphtheria. "He was canoeing and drank the water and died," Ernie says. "That's what I heard."

The Great Depression, sweeping through the world in the fall of 1929 just as swiftly as the influenza pandemic had eleven years earlier, was society's great equalizer. Perhaps the Roosevelts were immune, but the Colemans and millions of others were pushed to the edge. From there, they could see the frayed end of civilization. They had to act or fall.

Decisions were made. Frank stayed with his grandparents. Ernie would live with his mother, who found work as a nanny and housekeeper with a well-off family and moved into an upstairs apartment of their house. Just as Ernie had been too young to be aware of the presence and subsequent loss of his father, he can't remember Alfred Kyle first coming around. Alfred was one of nine brothers and one sister, a former navy man who served on the battleship *Iowa* as a fireman, shoveling coal into its boilers. Now he had a job at the Piano Works in East Rochester, forging the cast-iron plates on which the strings were mounted, then burnishing those plates with a polishing rouge to improve the instrument's internal aesthetics. Those pianos quickly left town, spreading music around the world.

Four years after George Coleman died, Alfred married May. With Ernie scurrying about at their feet, the couple moved to an apartment on the Commercial Street trolley line in downtown East Rochester, Alfred's hometown. It wasn't long before they bought a house on nearby Grant Street. Three bedrooms, two stories, a septic tank. The American dream was within reach for them, if it wasn't for the economic disaster that was suffocating the world.

"From '29 to '35, it was poverty time," Ernie says. "My mother found eighteen different ways to cook hamburger. We had a victory garden. My father had chickens on the property. There was a lot of bartering going on. Apparently, we had good production of eggs." Two big trees in the back provided apples to trade for other fruits and vegetables. Steaks were for the rich folks.

As he grew into a teenager and enrolled at East Rochester High School, sports was what mattered. Now the first real picture of Ernie, the competitor, emerges. As a tennis player, he had a secret weapon: he was ambidextrous. "I never had a backhand," he says. "I just switched the racket." In baseball, he was a catcher. "I couldn't hit at all; I was terrible," he says. But he recalls being a good defensive player with a good arm, throwing out many base runners trying to steal on him. The school had no hockey team until he and some friends put one together. Although the senior class at East Rochester had only about seventy-five kids, that was enough to field a football team. Everyone played both offense and defense. It was the leather helmet era; the forward pass was rarely explored territory. The teams moved on the ground like World War I armies facing each other across no-man's-land. Ernie was a 175-pound center, and on defense he took particular pride in rattling the opposite center with chatter about what he was going to do to him. "'I'm gonna climb over you,'" he says. "Next time, 'I'm gonna push you back.' They'd get so nervous, they couldn't pass the ball back."

That's right. Ernie Coleman was a trash talker. But the confident words failed him at inopportune times. "I had an inferiority complex with women," Ernie says. "I worried about what they thought of me." Throughout high school, he had only two dates. And as organizer of the junior prom and senior ball for the class of 1935, those dates were mandated. "It was protocol."

He hid from that insecurity by surrounding himself with two best friends. They called themselves the three musketeers. Ernie Coleman, Paul Smith, and Stan Corteville.

"We always did everything together," Ernie says. Sports, swimming in the barge canal, or downtown Rochester adventures to "browse around some of the stores and drool," he says. "We couldn't afford to buy anything." Yet movies at the RKO Palace on North Clinton and Loews Rochester at Clinton Avenue and Court Street—ornate, three thousand–seat theaters with chandeliers and winding staircases—were within their financial universe. Admission was fifteen cents, twenty-five cents after 6 p.m.

"We always got there early," Ernie says. "Absolutely."

So absolutely that, eight decades later, Ernie leaves the impression that he would still get to the movies early if it saved him a dime. During the Depression, that dime bought him one tiny burger at the White Castle knockoff of the day, White Tower Hamburgers. If the Musketeers were really feeling flush, they'd walk to an Italian restaurant on North Street, Catelli's, and load up on a twenty-cent plate of spaghetti. With one meatball, that's a nickel extra.

Ernie recalled these seemingly minor details as though they had happened just a few days ago—or as if he had pulled them from a hokey movie he'd watched last week. So I fact-checked him, reading through microfilms of newspapers from the 1930s. And there it was: admission to the RKO Palace, fifteen cents, twenty-five cents after 6 p.m.

This barren era demanded that Americans entertain themselves. Alfred Kyle not only made pianos, he played them. Ernie's house had an upright piano and Alfred had a pretty good voice. Ernie and his buddies—"No girls, just guys"—gathered for sing-alongs of the day's popular music that they heard on the radio. True, it was a while before they actually had a radio in the house. Until they could acquire a real one—which in the early 1920s was the financial equivalent of buying a used car—they listened on a crystal radio that Ernie built. A simple device requiring no outside power, it had a long antenna to pick up all available signals, a tuned circuit to select the signal, the crystal detector to process the signal, and earphones to hear it.

"You'd pick away, pick away, until you found a station and held it," Ernie says. That's how he and his stepfather listened to the 1927 Jack Dempsey–Gene Tunney heavyweight title fight.

"The one with the controversy," is how Ernie remembers it. The infamous "long count" fight in which Tunney may have benefited from a few extra seconds after a knockdown, allowing him to recover and win the match. This was real stepfather-son bonding. Alfred had boxed in the navy, and evidently brawled his way to the dinner table while growing up. "When you're one of nine boys," Ernie says, "you've got to learn how to handle yourself. He taught me some tricks."

In many ways this was a romantic vision of American life, but reality can be a gnawing hunger. The reality was that Ernie had to start bringing some money into the household. A next-door neighbor was an assistant golf pro and helped Ernie get his first job caddying at Locust Hill Country Club. In years to come, it would evolve into a championship course, for many years playing host to LPGA events. But when Ernie went to work there, it was less than ten years old, carved out of empty farmland in the suburb of Pittsford. Riding his bicycle five miles to the course, Ernie earned seventy-five cents carrying a set of bags for eighteen holes. On Saturdays, he doubled up and carried two bags. Maybe not such a big deal, Ernie concedes, since golfers back then used fewer clubs. The seventy-five cents—$1.50 on Saturdays—went into the family fund. As a bonus, while the golfers held court in the clubhouse over drinks, they'd let the caddies borrow their clubs to play.

"The golfers had their favorites," Ernie says, adding that one particular guy always asked for him. "I was happy to know I was doing a good job."

For Ernie, a new member of the country's workforce, the approval of others was important. He was happier still that the guy tipped well. But business setbacks were a constant threat throughout the Great Depression, even among the caddies. And during a tournament elsewhere, "he up and died on the golf course," Ernie says. "So I lost him."

Smart, hungry entrepreneurs like Ernie watched for opportunities to sell their services to what few families were still thriving in these hard times. A few times a week, he'd walk two miles from school to the home of the daughter of the family that employed his mother as a nanny. They needed a young guy like him to garden, trim trees, mow the lawn. Then he'd walk two miles home with the extra cash, which once again was deposited in the family fund.

That adolescent chase for cash ended the Monday after the East Rochester High School class of '35 graduation, when Ernie landed his first adult job. No more caddying or mowing. He was now a killer: a killer of silver foxes.

"The prime ones," Ernie says. They may have been amid a worldwide economic collapse, but rich women still loved to drape shimmering furs around their necks. Catching a car ride each day with the neighbor who had helped him get the job—Ernie was already a skilled networker—he was pulling in $15 a week for six days of work. The farm was home to five hundred foxes when Ernie arrived, and his job was simple at first.

"I was the guy that held them when they murdered them," he says. "Strychnine in the heart. One shot, they were dead." He'd flip the body to the skinner, who relieved the animals of their coats in the name of fashion. Then it was Ernie's duty to get rid of the bodies.

"It's amazing how small they were without their fur," he says. "They looked like little, tiny greyhounds." He buried them because "you couldn't use them for dog food. They had strychnine in them."

He was a failure at high school romance, but with foxes Ernie enjoyed better success in the reproductive sciences. The farm wanted to double the number of animals, and Ernie was assigned to monitor the breeding.

"There were three pairs we had to be very careful about," he says, "because the males would eat the pups. The minute we saw a fox was pregnant, we had to separate them."

Ernie's role in romancing the stoles must have been a success. The farm was soon up to about eight hundred foxes. Good work, although inspiring a mating frenzy in caged animals was likely not useful résumé material for his next career move, to a fireworks factory east of East Rochester. Now he was assembling skyrockets and Roman candles, a perfect fit for any young man's natural enthusiasm for explosives. The tools of this trade included a box with seventy-two slots in it, one sky-rocket per hole. He'd fill each one with the paper body, sift the gunpowder into the holes, pack an igniter pellet into each, then press the lid down tight. Ernie was particularly excited about the final step, testing the fireworks.

Oh, they worked all right, taking Ernie to new heights in the profession one afternoon. Each man assembling fireworks worked in his own little shed, for good reason: if there was an explosion, it wouldn't take down the entire operation.

"Everything was brass, I thought," Ernie says, "so I thought there would be no sparks." But as he tamped down the powder, a stray spark landed on Ernie's rack of fireworks. Realizing what was about to happen, he turned and ran, and his coworkers were treated to a surreal scene, Ernie says: "The door blew off and I was riding on it, like a magic carpet, they said. I didn't get hurt. Just tumbled into the grass, a little stunned."

Perhaps, he speculates, his ability to deal with the rough landing had something to do with one of the three musketeers' Depression-era moneymaking schemes. They'd created a tumbling team, putting on shows at the Rotary Club and during halftime at high-school basketball games. They choreographed the routines themselves.

The tumbling team, Ernie says, "taught me a lot about how to handle myself in the air."

Seemingly inconsequential experiences, such as the fearlessness that comes with defying gravity, served Ernie well over the years.

Surviving the fireworks episode, Ernie moved on to the Merchants Despatch Transportation Company, refurbishing refrigerated railroad cars. The men stripped the cars of their timber frames, setting aside the wood for anyone who wanted it.

"Of course, it was full of nails," Ernie says. "So you had to pull nails."

Much of this abandoned lumber went into building the shambling summer homes perched on the edge of Lake Ontario in an eight-street community that was called White City then, sometimes referred to as Tent City, after the white canvas of the tents that lined the neighborhood. As the homes took on a more permanent status, the town would assume the resort-sounding name of Summerville.

* * *

A couple of years out of high school and as an ambitious workingman, Ernie acquired his first car by borrowing $25 from his grandmother,

"Because my folks didn't have any money," he says. It was a green 1926 Chevy, used, "with bald tires and no side skirts." Ernie gave his grandmother $2.50 a week until the loan was paid off.

An obvious pattern emerges during these Depression days: a continual shuffling from job to job. "The jobs evaporated," Ernie says. "You had to."

It was the same for his brother, who bought canoes and rented them at Mendon Ponds Park. That didn't work. People spent their recreation money with restraint, and the quiet of a canoe pond excursion couldn't compete with the crowds at Ontario Beach and Sea Breeze Amusement Park with the wooden Jack Rabbit roller coaster and huge Danceland ballroom dominated by a ceiling mirror ball.

Frank abandoned wilderness amusements in favor of driving through Monroe County in his Model T sedan, selling laundry detergent for ten cents a bottle. Their stepfather Alfred wasn't immune to the job shuffle. When he was laid off from the Piano Works in 1937, May would have nothing to do with welfare. Her husband soon took a job, at $9 a week, with the Public Works Administration, Franklin Roosevelt's massive make-work program for the millions of unemployed. Alfred built trails and small buildings in Mendon Ponds Park until a few years later, when he returned to the Piano Works, laboring in the building's power plant. He was back at the bottom, shoveling coal into the building's boilers, just as he had on the *Iowa*, slowly moving up the job ladder until he retired many years later.

When Ernie's railroad car rehab work dried up, he was fine with the unemployment cash. His first check was for $21. "That was big money there, for doing nothing," he says. Like the price of a movie ticket, decades later he's still carrying around seemingly insignificant figures in his head: seventy-five cents to carry a rich man's golf bag, $15 a week to kill foxes, that 10-cent hamburger. It was the Depression, and every dime was important.

Ernie was competitive, but he was also forward looking. The unemployment money gave him the chance to take classes in operating lathing and planing equipment at the college downtown, the grandly named Rochester Athenaeum and Mechanics Institute. It later became Rochester Institute of Technology, and by 1968, as was the case with many people and businesses, it had fled to the suburbs.

"At that time, I had been hounding Gleason Works," Ernie says. Gleason Works, even into the twenty-first century, was a long, oddly elegant factory sprawling a couple of blocks along Rochester's University Avenue. Back then, the company's major function was cutting gears for heavy military armaments. After his short period of unemployment and college courses, early in 1938 Ernie was hired as a Gleason Works machinist, working the gear-cutting machinery for sixty-five cents an hour.

Just as the jobs had been racing through his hands, other aspects of Ernie's life were accelerating as well. His mother was ill. Peritonitis, it was at first thought, an inflammation of the abdominal wall.

"They didn't know what it was," Ernie says. "They opened her up, saw what it was, closed her up, that was it. It was just a matter of time." Colon cancer claimed her a few months later.

And as if making up for lost time, the kid who couldn't talk to girls at East Rochester High School now had a girlfriend, Ruth Naramore. Life was looking up as the Depression faded from the landscape. World War II had erupted, and the U.S. economy benefited from the chaos, manufacturing goods and weapons for other people's battles. "I was always optimistic," Ernie says. "I could see it getting better."

The war and Ruth were two conflicts that Ernie didn't see coming his way.

FOUR

Rochester is no longer the thriving town that it was when George and Clara Coleman arrived from England. It has grown, but like many eastern cities in the final decade of the twentieth century, Rochester struggled with the loss of its manufacturing base, the remains of much of it an ethereal archaeology of abandoned buildings and vegetation-covered foundations along the Genesee River. Yet a million people still lived and worked in Monroe County by the end of the millennium, and the glow from the city's lights obscures the stars at night. Sail a few miles into Lake Ontario, and many more stars become apparent. The Milky Way emerges as a thin veil of cosmic clutter tracing its way across the sky, the edge of our galaxy.

Ernie saw the northern lights here so many times that he was a bit bored with the shimmering curtain of greens, blues, and whites. "I haven't looked for that in five years," he says. Watching the sky over Lake Ontario, Ernie was more interested in a fleeting natural phenomenon that can be more elusive: the dot of green that sometimes appears on the top edge of the sun as it dips below the horizon. It's the refraction of higher frequency light—green—traveling along the thinner edge of the upper atmosphere after the curvature of Earth itself has obstructed the yellows and reds of the sun moving through the lower, denser atmosphere. The prism effect lasts one or two seconds, and it is tiny.

Some longtime sailors, seemingly steady fellows, will tell you they've observed other unexplained lights in the night sky. In his more than seventy years on the lake, Ernie says he's never spotted anything that might have been alien spacecraft. Why would they be coming here? In his practical mind, Ernie reasons that we don't have anything that interplanetary beings could possibly need.

Lake Ontario is the smallest in area of the five Great Lakes, but shallower Lake Erie is smaller by volume. Huron, Michigan, and Superior are much larger, although sailors will tell you that the two small, shallow-bottomed lakes are more easily riled when difficult weather rolls in. From a distance Ernie has watched waterspouts, the tornado-like funnel clouds over the lake. Although they are much weaker than tornadoes over land, reports of waterspouts damaging boats do exist, particularly boats tied to their piers, so from a distance is the safe way to watch them.

Sailors must be mindful of other dangers. High in the mast, most sailboats display a radar reflector, a volleyball-sized octahedron with several reflecting surfaces, a better target for a large ship's radar. Big freighters and tankers share the water with pleasure boats, and though accidents are rare, they happen. In 2006, off England's Isle of Wight, a yacht named *Ouzo* and its crew of three were lost when it either collided with a large ferry or perhaps was swamped by the ferry's wake. Ernie's been as close as seventy-five yards to a big lake freighter.

"Scary," he says. "Those suckers can't stop. You see that thing coming up, with the bow wave swinging along."

For many long minutes after spotting a ship on the horizon, a sailboat can't be certain where the bigger vessel is heading. "Finally, I realized if you see both sides of a ship"—the bow and the stern—"you're safe," Ernie says. If you see only the bow, that's not good. It's coming toward you.

But the most common danger is the unexpected storm. Ernie sailed through some big ones, and he'd even seen the static electricity that can envelop a boat. They call it St. Elmo's fire, a whitish-blue wave of light lasting only four to five seconds, "running and dancing up and down the rigging," Ernie says. "It's very bad for the instruments." Ernie recalls a race in which four boats lost their speed indicators, radios, and depth sounders. "The whole works—just wiped it all out." Caught in one such storm of electrified atmosphere, he saw the antenna for his own radio navigation system, "start humming like a bumblebee. A big bumblebee." Ernie yelled for one of his crew to quickly turn it off, saving the equipment. Sailing is a sport, a recreation, a relaxing afternoon, but many occasions arise when the crew must think quickly.

* * *

After more than seven decades of racing, it was long past time for Ernie to slow down. He had been through a handful of boats, but since 1975 settled in with *Desire*, a Columbia 26. The name came to him in a dream. At twenty-six feet long, *Desire* was big enough to handle the fifty-two-mile crossing to Canada. It is a cruising boat, not a racer. But "the boat doesn't know that," Ernie says.

"I've seen strong winds, lots of rain. I've been in forty-mile winds in that boat," he says. Ernie often found himself matched against boats faster than *Desire*. But that was fine, because boats are assigned handicaps in the world of lake racing. These events aren't the America's Cup, in which the multimillionaire with the latest equipment wins. The races are a test of the sailors, not the boats. And to the slowest can come the spoils.

Ernie recalls a day in which he and another Columbia 26 were rated the weakest boats in the race. The two eased along, trailing far behind the rest of the pack. The hares had all crossed the finish line when the wind suddenly picked up—blowing a real stink, in sailor language—and scooted the two Columbia 26s along quickly enough, which, with their handicaps factored in, resulted in a one-two finish for the tortoises. Slow and steady can indeed win the race.

That was Ernie's life philosophy as well. At least that's what he said. Friends and family members knowingly smile about the simmering competitive edge that emerged in Ernie during races. But at age ninety, still driving a car, Ernie tells of being amused by other drivers' displays of impatience at intersections. "What's the hurry?" he asks. "Where are you going? What time are you going to save, two minutes? I think that has had a lot to do with my success in racing. Take your time, look around. Look where the other guy is. Get to know the speed of your boat. It's all experience. I've been racing for seventy-one years, and I can't recall two races that were the same."

Typical of such atypical sails was a Rochester Yacht Club annual Fourth of July cruise across the lake in the mid-1990s to Cobourg, Ontario. "The wind was out of the west, very strong," Ernie says. It started with three-foot waves and then a storm warning: all small boats take refuge. *Desire*, with Ernie and Marilyn aboard, was far beyond the midpoint of Lake Ontario by then. "Am I supposed to put the thing on my shoulder and go home?" Ernie laughs.

He can laugh about it now. Then, they were sailing the trough between eight-foot waves. "I told Marilyn, 'Don't look back,'" Ernie says. She would have seen that the waves were higher than the boat. He was calculating what arrangement of sails would slow *Desire*, which sail he could let out while still retaining enough speed to steer the boat rather than allowing the lake do with it what it would. He also was calculating how to limit damage to the boat, if it came to that. Which sail he would prefer to sacrifice. "I let the main out, spilled some wind," Ernie says. "What cost more, the main or the jib? I let the jib out. The boat was shaking like a leaf. I was afraid the boat would shake apart."

They were the last to arrive in port. *Desire* was still under full sail a mere two hundred feet from the Cobourg harbor entrance before Ernie dared take down the main and limp into the dock on his motor. A dramatic arrival, and the other sailors hooted in mock approval. "Little did they know," Ernie says of *Desire*'s charge into the harbor, "I couldn't do anything about it." It wasn't classic textbook sailing, but Ernie never had a formal class. He sailed on instinct. "It just came naturally," he says. "I guess I inherited it from my grandfather. Incidentally, I'm still learning."

Mastering sailing techniques can fill a lifetime. It starts with the sails and the telltale, a strip of fabric attached to the aft edge of the mainsail, the largest sail on the boat. If the telltale is streaming backward, you're fine. The jib, the triangular sail set at the front of the mast, is generally outfitted with telltales as well. If any of the telltales begin spinning and fluttering, that tells the sailor the wind isn't hitting the sails properly, and the boat must be edged over a bit in that direction. "Sail trim"—adjusting the sails—"is the motor of the boat," Ernie says. "The better you trim it, the faster you go."

The wind was once the only way to move a boat such distances. Sails were a necessity. Not anymore. But still, the silence after the motor goes off and the sails go up draws sailors like Ernie out onto the lake. "It was the thrill of being on water, under motion with no noise," he says. "I loved it. I still love it. We'd go out, and I couldn't wait to get the motor turned off."

The motor. That's the enemy. Most sailboat owners are dismissive of powerboats. They call them "stinkpots."

Destination rarely matters. Unlike the landscape, which quickly fades into a dull green line off the stern, the seascape shifts with each voyage onto the lake. There is no truer line than the horizon of a large body of water. Yet the water surface changes. The wind changes. Friends would say, "'Where'd you go?'" Ernie says. "'Back and forth, four or five miles.' We can really relax out there."

Out there a sailor can hear the cry of seabirds, the wind catching the sail, the slap of water against the hull, or the metallic tap, tap, tap of the lines against the aluminum mast. But mostly, there's silence. This is a time for thinking—or not thinking.

"Nothing," Ernie says of what passes through his mind at such moments. "Just plain enjoying. I'm always watching the sail, to trim it. It's just my nature."

Also in his nature: "If there's another boat out there, he's racing," Ernie says. "Whether he knows it or not."

FIVE

As 1933 drew to a close, the Bethlehem Shipping Company's Fore River plant in Quincy, Massachusetts, was preparing to begin work on the last of the seven ships that later would be named the New Orleans class of heavy cruisers. This one would be USS *Vincennes*. The keel was laid on January 2, 1934, and, over the next three years, the ship would grow to 588 feet long, 61 feet and 10 inches wide, its eight boilers and four propellers capable of moving it along at about thirty-two knots. Miss Harriett Virginia Kimmell, daughter of the mayor of Vincennes, Indiana, was brought east to preside over the launching ceremony of the still-incomplete shell.

The war machine that she christened amid the flags and bunting and social events that surrounded the occasion would soon be fitted with a main battery of nine eight-inch guns mounted in three triple turrets, each gun capable of firing a 355-pound shell 31,700 yards—eighteen miles—and piercing five inches of armor plate. A crew of 952 officers and enlisted men would tend to the needs of this ship. With Europe still sifting through the ruins of World War I and aching from memories of the devastation that explosives and steel could do to servicemen and civilians alike, this class of warship was designed within the limitations of the Washington Naval Treaty of 1921 and the later London Naval Treaty. The U.S. Navy intended to match it against one potential opponent in particular: a ship of the same heavy cruiser category manned by a Japanese crew.

As *Vincennes* emerged from the drawing board in 1933, so did six-teen-year-old Ernie's first boat in the garage of his family's home in East Rochester. He had examined photos of sailboats closely, assembling a tiny paper prototype whose performance was satisfying. Why wouldn't a scaled-up version work as well?

"I had help from my stepfather," Ernie says. "He was a pretty good carpenter, although he never pursued it as a trade."

Ernie himself cut out the rudder in shop class. The finished boat was twelve feet long, four feet wide, flat bottomed with slightly curving sides. "And heavy, quite heavy," Ernie says.

He and fellow musketeer Paul Smith hauled the boat to nearby Canan-daigua Lake, launched it, and sailed downwind about a mile before decid-ing to turn back.

Ernie was a self-taught shipwright. Perhaps seeking the advice of a knowledgeable crowd would have been in order. Lacking a proper keel, the boat was simply pushed sideways by any wind gusting in from the side. The two boys herded it back to the beach and walked it home like a dog on a leash. "I gave it to a neighbor," Ernie says. "He turned it into a fishing boat."

His first attempt to answer the call of the wind and waves had come to an ignominious end, a pile of lumber in the shape of a boat now sentenced to plodding through the rocks and algae of the lakeshore in the search for brown trout. Ernie never even had the opportunity to give the boat a proper name.

"I gave it a lot of names because it wouldn't sail," Ernie concedes. "But that was different."

That wouldn't be the end of his sailing ambitions. His DNA wouldn't allow it. But more likely, as I was beginning to suspect after a few weeks of conversations with Ernie, it was the times, this era of hardship that forged the Greatest Generation. The era produced its share of scoundrels, thieves, scam artists, drunks, and serial killers, but if you were a clever guy like Ernie, you could thrive in a landscape of limited resources.

Environment, being in the right place at the right time, certainly played a role as well. Perhaps Ernie would not have moved beyond the casual interest of any kid building model sailboats out of balsa wood, and past the failure of his first boat, were it not for Canandaigua Lake and the constant presence of the sailboats skipping along its waves. At eleven-and-a-half miles long and one-and-a-half miles wide, Canandaigua is the fourth largest of the Finger Lakes, long traces of fresh water spread out like the fingers of a pair of giant hands resting on the rural landscape of central and western New York. The lakes were created by a series of glacial movements beginning two million years ago in the Pleistocene era, ice sheets more than two miles deep descending from Hudson Bay.

In 1932, about eleven thousand years after the last of these glaciers had retreated deep into Canada, Ernie's parents paid $100 for a lot at Crystal Beach, about seven miles down the east side of Canandaigua Lake. On that land, working on weekends throughout the summer, Ernie, Frank, and their stepfather built a cottage.

Now Ernie was tantalizingly close to the water. Sailboats scooted up and down the lake all around him. He wanted to join them. Sailing skipped a generation in the Coleman family, bounding from George to Ernie over his two fathers. Ernie's biological father may have grown up on a Thames sailing barge, but he had chosen the stability of a drafting board before his life was cut short. Ernie's stepfather actually did have a boat, but to Ernie that one didn't measure up. It was a small one with a motor, for fishing only.

"He was an enthusiastic fisherman," Ernie says, without showing any enthusiasm for the sport himself; remember, he considered his first boat-building project to be a failure after it ended up as a mere carp trawler. And Ernie never had any interest in fish, unless it was dinnertime. To Ernie, the water was never about what lies beneath.

His flat-bottomed, keel-less disaster had been the first attempt. Ernie waited nearly two years before the next opportunity presented itself. It came unexpectedly with one of his high school graduation presents: a leftover canoe from his brother's failed Mendon Ponds Park business.

It was the wrong kind of craft, as far as Ernie was concerned, and in rough shape. But just as he had learned the principles of carpentry while helping to build the family summer cottage, the cottage project had also sharpened his resourcefulness. To get the materials to build the house, the family had borrowed the milkman's truck to move lumber from where many people in East Rochester were getting it during the Great Depression: rummaging through the rough piles ripped from the railcars being rebuilt at the Merchants Despatch Transportation Company.

Ernie's second sailboat was the product of a similar creative spirit. He mounted a ten-foot mast with a boom to the bottom of the canoe, fashioning a sail from an old bedsheet. Maybe a little top-heavy, but "I was the ballast," Ernie says. He steered with a paddle. If the wind died away completely, he used the paddle to get back home. A neighbor gave him a leeboard—a plank that fits on the side of the boat, enabling it to sail into the wind, something lacking in the first homebuilt craft that he had been forced to walk home on its maiden voyage. Leeboards are not unknown in American sailing waters, but they're not particularly common. They were, however, quite frequently seen on Thames sailing barges.

This boat worked. "I used to sail that thing all over the place," Ernie says. But it was just a first successful step. A neighbor had a fourteen-foot dinghy stored in a shed, an International 14, often called a cat boat, and offered to sell it to Ernie. The asking price was $75. Ernie didn't have that kind of money, but the neighbor turned the boat over to him anyway.

"He said 'give me $5 whenever you can find it,'" Ernie says.

After about $25 in payments, the neighbor called it a done deal.

The dinghy was a problematic acquisition. "It leaked like a sieve, it was so dry," Ernie says. The boat was of lapstrake construction, with overlapping curved planks built up from the keel, and a mast set at the forward end. Enlisting the help of the seemingly always available Smith—the third musketeer, Corteville, had been enjoying success with girls that escaped the other two—Ernie set about the tedious task of re-riveting the entire boat and pouring varnish into the cracks.

The rehab was a success. The boat sailed well, but it wasn't quite the right fit for Ernie. The competitor in Ernie wanted to race those other guys chasing the Canandaigua Lake winds. But boats race against each other in categories established by governing bodies in much the same way that the capabilities of the warships of the time were governed by naval treaties. Each sailboat category bears specific limitations on size, weight, and sails. And there, Ernie had the wind taken from his sails: his boat was too old. The local sporting world had passed it by. No one was racing International 14s around western New York anymore.

Ernie's racing career was inhibited by other new developments: the cottage that the three musketeers had rented in the summer of 1937, the high school sorority that had moved into the cabin next door, and the nearby dance hall. He was finished with high school, but Ernie was suddenly doing quite well in chemistry with Ruth. "Things went off pretty well; all of a sudden, pow! The fact I was so self-conscious in high school," he says, his voice trailing off. "The fact that a girl paid so much attention to me, I was taken over."

Ernie was falling for the first girl who'd ever paid attention to him.

* * *

On Irondequoit Bay, a natural harbor formed by Lake Ontario pushing its way into the shoreline, the boat that everyone was chasing was a new design. A simple, fifteen-and-a-half foot, two-man dinghy called the Snipe. Three of them had arrived from California and dominated the local races. By 1936, just five years after it had been designed and the first one built, the Snipe had become the most popular racing class in the world.

Ernie had been romancing Ruth with boat rides, a whirlwind romance that would too quickly lead to marriage less than a year later in March 1938. The couple lived with his parents until Ernie's brother—now managing a seed company—told him that the other unit was available in the Marion Street duplex where he lived with his wife and young son, just a few blocks from Gleason Works. Good enough for a newly married couple.

But Ernie was already discovering three things that maybe he should have thought about before his first girlfriend swept him up like a sailboat before the wind. One, Ruth liked to talk—far more than Ernie liked to listen. Two, she really wasn't interested in sailing. And three, he needed one of those new boats to get into the racing scene.

Ernie's solution—his solution to two of those three problems, anyway—was to buy a Snipe kit. Once again he went to work in the garage of his parents' Grant Street house, where he had room to spread out the boat parts—and room for himself.

"It didn't amount to much," he recalls. "Just a frame."

And, he confesses, "It was kind of an out for me, to get away from Ruth."

With the completion of the Snipe, which he named *Kiddo*, Ernie was now on equal footing with his new sailing friends at the bay's Newport Yacht Club. Better footing, actually, as the races unfolded. While Ruth was ashore, socializing with the other wives and girlfriends, the inexperienced Ernie was actually winning. He was collecting trophies, his success preventing him from incorporating the mistakes of others into his own sailing style.

"I knew nothing about racing," he says. "I was so far ahead, I never learned there's rules of the road."

The old road, it turns out, was the wrong direction. Ernie's boat was faster because it was lighter. Rather than tying his boat to the pier after the race, he'd built himself a haul-out, cranking *Kiddo* out of the water to dry after each outing.

"All of their boats soaked up water and had growth on them," Ernie says. "Here I come down with a free boat. Well, they were no match for me."

His competitors now wanted boats whose hulls were as smooth as the sides of a brown trout, and they were willing to pay for it.

"Before the summer was out," Ernie says, "I built a haul-out for every boat."

But that wasn't the only secret. He'd outfitted the Snipe with a dagger-board—today more commonly called a centerboard—a blade-like retractable keel that gives a small sailboat more stability and enables it to make its way upwind more easily. It's not a new invention. In 2008, a couple of shipwreck hunters found a fifty-five-foot schooner equipped with a daggerboard on the bottom of Lake Ontario, ten miles off the southern coast. Ernie and thousands of other sailors had probably passed peacefully over that piece of history many times after it sank in the early 1800s.

When the other Newport Yacht Club sailors picked up on Ernie's daggerboard, many of them wanted one as well. Ernie traced out a pattern, took it to a salvage yard, and had a handful of daggerboards cut from scrap steel. He took the roughed-out shapes home to the Marion Street duplex, lugged them down to the basement, and ground the edges with equipment borrowed from Gleason Works.

He'd also tucked away a box of old fireworks beneath the basement steps from his days at the fireworks factory, maybe a hundred colorful explosives. Ernie and his brother were grinding away at a daggerboard when a shower of sparks landed in the box.

"I dove into the coal bin," Ernie says. "He went under a table."

The box went off in a series of percussive echoes. Ruth was not amused.

"I didn't make any brownie points that day," Ernie says. "The whole house smelled of fireworks."

That was a Saturday evening. The next afternoon, Ernie and Frank had moved the grinding operation out to the backyard.

"It was a nice day," Ernie recalls. A December Sunday. Frank's wife was inside the house with the radio on.

"She hollered out," as Ernie remembers it, "'The Japanese are bombing Pearl Harbor!'"

SIX

That December morning, *Vincennes* was already at war, with Hitler and nature. During the year, the ship had been engaged in a series of training exercises and neutrality patrols in the Caribbean Sea and the North Atlantic Ocean, undeclared battlegrounds where German U-boats were stalking cargo ships heavily laden with Franklin D. Roosevelt's "Arsenal of Democracy." The weapons and supplies served as an intravenous lifeline directly into England, which was now virtually alone after the fall of France. Those cargoes likely included armored vehicles, aircraft, and cannon, whose inner workings featured the precision gears that Ernie had helped manufacture at Gleason Works.

American neutrality knew no boundaries. As the Japanese planes appeared over Pearl Harbor in the morning sky, it was already early evening off the coast of South Africa, where *Vincennes* was a part of the U.S. Navy escort for Convoy WS-12X, American transports carrying British troops. The ships were fighting through a fierce gale, with nearly every cruiser and destroyer sustaining some damage. On *Vincennes*, a motor whaleboat was smashed and a Curtiss SOC Seagull floatplane was torn from the deck, the waves slapping it against the catapult silos and hangar doors like a cat with a yarn toy before sweeping it over the side. This likely felt rough enough, until word began to arrive of what had happened on the other side of the world at Pearl Harbor.

For most Americans, the war had been a distant transmission, something filed by foreign correspondents for newspapers and magazines and on radio, TV, and the Pathé newsreels of the day shown in movie theaters before the main feature. This was a big year for movies, with *Citizen Kane*, *The Maltese Falcon*, *Dumbo*, and Alfred Hitchcock's *Suspicion* all onscreen in 1941. The effect on military recruiting leveled by one of the most popular films of the year, Bud Abbott and Lou Costello's *Buck Privates*, is open for debate.

"There was a war and we were concerned about the Allies," Ernie says. "We kept track of it. Hitler did a number on Europe and the bombing of London. We were squeezing for the Allies to stop him. The assassination of the Jews, that was horrible. Now they're trying to say that didn't happen."

Modern-day deniers aside, the Holocaust was indeed happening. Hitler was invading the Soviet Union, and Ernie suspected that the United States would be drawn into the European war. But he was shocked when the first move was made by Japan.

"Oh yes, absolutely," he says. "They really took us by total surprise. If they followed up, they could have captured the Hawaiian Islands. We didn't have much of a force there."

Now the United States was fully engaged in a world war. Unless you were employed by Gleason Works.

"Anybody in the war effort, making stuff for World War II, was exempt," Ernie says. "You were 4-F."

But just because a guy was 4-F didn't mean he couldn't read the newspapers or see the newsreels before the start of the movies. The Japanese had pushed the U.S. forces out of the Philippines. The Germans were massing troops on the coast of France, staring across the English Channel, and driving tanks through the African desert alongside the Italians. Men would be needed. Men like Frank. Selling seeds wasn't vital to the war effort.

Ernie began to think. His brother was married with a young child. If he joined the service, maybe they would leave Frank out of the war. It was an interesting scheme, selfless for sure.

"I didn't tell him that," Ernie says.

And it wasn't the entire truth. In March 1942, "I called my draft board and told them I wanted to volunteer with the navy," he says. "I joined the navy, naturally, because I'm a sailor. I wanted to do my effort, to be a good American citizen. I also wanted to seek some adventure."

And he wanted to escape the war on the home front.

"I wasn't getting along too well at home," Ernie says. "My wife was a social climber, and I'm not."

The monotony of Gleason Works, the Imperial Japanese Navy, and Ruth were too much for one man to handle.

"I wanted to get away," Ernie says. "Sailing wasn't enough."

* * *

Perhaps Pearl Harbor taught the Pentagon a lesson about giving its enemies easy access to military assets, because in the spring 1942, when the navy decided it needed a new base to handle all of the fresh-faced kids signing up, it started bulldozing one into the hillsides around Seneca Lake, just a few hours' drive from Rochester. But Sampson Naval Base wasn't ready when Ernie passed his physical, so he was mustered out to the Great Lakes Naval Training Station, the huge, self-supporting facility on the west shore of Lake Michigan, north of Chicago, a thousand miles from the closest ocean. Before Pearl Harbor, it had been supporting 10,000 navy men. In the year after the attack, the training station exploded, handling seventy-five thousand recruits, most bound for the Pacific.

"I didn't know what was in store for me," Ernie says.

If he had been paying attention during *Buck Privates*, he would have known it was boot camp, starting with calisthenics at 6 a.m., then classes in aircraft recognition and navy regulations.

"No gun training; they just explained it all," Ernie says. "All of the firearms were in service." Most importantly, "There's a right way and the navy way," they were told. "You do it the navy way."

They learned the navy way for three weeks—shorter than the usual stint but bodies were needed—followed by a week's furlough at home. Back in Rochester, Ernie was nothing special as he walked around in his uniform. A lot of the guys were doing it. "Everyone said, 'It's a good place to be from,'" Ernie says. "'A long way from.'"

Soon enough, they got their wish for adventure, trading the humdrum of hometown for exotic-sounding place names on a map such as Bataan, Morocco, and the Aleutian Islands. "Off to war," Ernie says. Three days on a train across America.

"We spent most of it on sidings, I think," he says, until the last stop: Pleasanton, California. Sixty miles east of San Francisco. This was the newly activated Camp Shoemaker, a vast tract of wood barracks that was a part of the navy's rapidly evolving Fleet City, three landlocked bases lying side by side that served as the gateway to the war for many sailors.

Here, Ernie ran headlong into the classic military oxymoron, "hurry up and wait."

"You muster in at 8 a.m.," he says. "If your name wasn't on the list, you had until the next morning."

For Ernie, this went on for weeks, plenty of time for the average sailor to get himself embroiled in a handful of situations not addressed in *The Bluejacket's Manual*, the basic handbook for U.S. sailors. He was twenty-five years old, older than a lot of these kids waiting for their assignments, and Ernie's curiosity ran a little deeper than the USO dances.

"I was very interested in history. I wasn't a typical sailor, find the first bar," he says. He explored, riding trains and buses to San Jose and Berkeley. He stopped at museums, took in the scenery, wandered out to the wharf and San Francisco's fishing village, inspected an old sailing ship tied to the pier. He rode the trolley to the beach, which he remembered as "loaded with seagulls and scals. They had a museum showing the fish that were caught off the pier that was there, various artifacts that were a part of San Francisco."

He was a tourist, but trouble did find him. Late one night in San Francisco, alone, waiting for a bus, Ernie was confronted by three zoot suiters. Young guys in outrageous long coats with oversized shoulders, long key chains, porkpie hats, and baggy peg-leg trousers. The sailors had been warned about them.

"They were against the war," Ernie says. "They attacked me on a corner." Fortunately, it was a construction site with lumber lying about, and the future carpenter knew a few uses for a two-by-four besides wall studs. He picked up a board and began nailing one of the zoot suiters.

"Needless to say, they backed off, yelling obscenities," Ernie says.

It was his first hand-to-hand combat during the war. And Ernie had acquitted himself well. Even at age ninety-three, when I'd first met Ernie and was sizing him up, I could tell that he must have been one tough character. You can spot those guys. They're not all twitchy; they have a real physical presence. Their movements are confident, economical. Subsequent decades of wielding a hammer and pushing newly framed walls into place had honed the muscles and tendons in his forearms, back, and legs. Looking at that small and powerful yet aging frame, I could tell that strength had always been there.

In routing the zoot suiters, Ernie unwittingly had been caught up in a battle of cultures originating on the West Coast in the 1930s in racial tension between whites and Mexican immigrants. The whites accused the Mexican immigrants of taking jobs from them, a familiar battle cry even into the twenty-first century. By wartime, the confrontation frequently was seen as patriotic by the whites, who interpreted the flamboyant zoot suits as a deliberate flouting of war rationing, since wool was one of the early items to be rationed by the War Production Board, resulting in conservatively cut fashions. By 1943, the zoot suit culture had expanded to include both blacks and Mexican Americans, who frequently scuffled with the predominantly white sailors of the West Coast.

This bad alchemy exploded in Los Angeles during a series of nights when gangs of sailors and civilians marched the streets, beating up any zoot suiters they could get their hands on, often tearing off their zoot suits and burning them in the streets. Some people saw these avenging sailors as patriots cleaning up Los Angeles. But the true nature of the movement was clear; a committee established to study the riots immediately after the fighting had ended determining that the conflict was fueled by racism.

Yet, in telling the story years later, Ernie makes no mention of the zoot suiters' race. If it had mattered at all to him back then, their race was no longer worth mentioning for this ninety-three-year-old sailor. They were just weirdly outfitted guys who were against the war.

* * *

Not long after his brush with the zoot suiters, Ernie checked the 8 a.m. assignment sheet, and there it was. His name. Coleman, Ernest. He was being dispatched to Treasure Island, in the San Francisco Bay, to catch an army transport ship to Hawaii. Five days cramped alongside fellow servicemen. And to occupy their time?

"Nothing," Ernie says. "You're just a passenger. It was a rough ride, a lot of guys got real seasick. I mean, bad, bad."

This is one of the few times when a specific detail fails Ernie. He does not remember the name of the ship, but he did hear later that it was torpedoed and sunk somewhere off Australia.

In Hawaii came more days of waiting and a chance to see Honolulu. Ernie was a tourist once again, heading into the city with his alphabet buddy, a navy postmaster named Richard Bennett.

"Everyone went by their last name in the navy," Ernie says. "Everything was run by the alphabet. He was 'B'; I was 'C.'"

Ernie recalls touring the Aloha Tower with its spectacularly huge German-built clock weighing seven tons, one of the largest clocks in the United States or any of its territories. A grand hotel was nearby, and the building's management offered it to the navy men as a proper venue for their homecoming. "The boys would come back from a submarine strike, and they'd turn the hotel over to them," Ernie says. "Boy, what they'd do to that hotel, you wouldn't believe. But those boys were under pressure."

Yes, it was sometimes better to forget this was war. Until the reminder posted on the barracks wall at 8 a.m. the next morning: "A . . . B . . . C . . . Coleman, Ernest."

He finally had his ship. A heavy cruiser, USS *Vincennes*.

SEVEN

Six months after the Japanese attack, salvage operations at Pearl Harbor had been startlingly effective. A bus filled with thirty new sailors, including Ernie, followed the road into Pearl, where the wrecked aircraft had been swept away and five battleships and two cruisers had been pulled from the harbor mud. However, the capsized *Oklahoma* was still lying like a turtle in Battleship Row. Likewise, the bombed and burned-out battleship *Arizona* was where the Japanese planes had left it, the same place it sits today as a national monument. It was estimated that fifteen hundred sailors' bodies were still in those two ships in the summer of 1942. Many remain in *Arizona* to this day.

By the time Ernie arrived, *Arizona*'s collapsed forward tripod mast and bridge would have been cut away. Still in place were the mainmast, the stern—slightly above the waves—and the ship's big guns, each fifty feet long. In *Arizona*'s twenty-six-year history, the guns had never been fired in wartime, unlike those of the ship on which Ernie was aboard, now leaving the harbor. *Arizona* had been reduced to a symbol of another nation's treachery as the United States went to war.

Ernie shakes his head no when, seventy years later, he's asked if he saw any of this blackened Pearl Harbor wreckage, including this ship that had been the star attraction in the Pathé newsreels, with photos of its burning carcass featured prominently in recruiting stations across the country as well. Perhaps *Vincennes* didn't pass close enough; perhaps Ernie was on the wrong side of the ship or below deck. Perhaps he didn't wish to see it, or had forgotten it, or wanted to forget it.

If the remains of that terrible December morning were still visible as *Vincennes* left the harbor, for Ernie it had disappeared into that black hole where we put pain.

"The barracks were way out of the way," he says. "Honolulu itself is a long way from Pearl Harbor. I was too busy getting acquainted with the ship, finding where my berth was."

In photos, *Vincennes* appears to be quite a pretty ship if you disregard the deadly intent of its design. Perhaps its lines looked too busy just aft of amidships, with its two scout seaplanes and their cranes and catapults. *Vincennes* wasn't muscular looking like so many warships. It was lean like a greyhound. And it had a war record. First dodging German U-boats in the Atlantic and Caribbean, then transferring to the Pacific in time to participate in one of the most ambitious schemes during the early months of the war: helping to escort the aircraft carrier *Hornet* to within bombing range of Japan. From there, on the morning of April 16, 1942, still 650 miles from their target, Jimmy Doolittle's sixteen B-25 bombers left *Hornet* and dropped a handful of bombs on the island nation. Little damage was done, but the United States had demonstrated that Japan was not safely beyond the range of the war.

After that mission, the busy *Vincennes* arrived too late to participate in the Battle of Coral Sea in early May, but a month later it was a part of the most important naval action of the Pacific War: the Battle of Midway, where, on June 4, U.S. carrier-based planes sank four Japanese carriers. *Vincennes* was assigned to the force protecting the American carriers, its antiaircraft batteries credited with shooting down one Japanese dive-bomber, although enough Japanese planes breached the defense to severely damage the aircraft carrier *Yorktown*, which was finished off by a torpedo from a Japanese submarine. *Vincennes* sustained some damage itself, requiring a return to Pearl Harbor for repairs.

In early July *Vincennes* was once again bound for battle. Ernie had known coming into this adventure that the assignment he did not want was the firerooms, feeding the ship's boilers, where the temperature could reach 140 degrees. His stepfather had worked that hell on *Iowa*. Instead Ernie applied for a position as carpenter's mate, and he got the job. To the navy, that meant more studying, more tests.

"How to hold a hammer," Ernie says, that sort of obvious thing. "There was always a carpenter's shop on a ship, and I enjoyed doing it." The navy was his vocational school. Like the Rochester Athenaeum and

Mechanics Institute, but with eight-inch guns. Ernie was calculating where this might lead after the war. "I might get to be a carpenter and get paid for it," he says. "Wages were very good for the carpenters." So Ernie's duties as *Vincennes* left Hawaii hardly would be any threat to the Japanese.

"Chipping paint, stripping the deck, chipping more paint," he says. "It was a steel hull, the saltwater rusted it pretty bad."

Ernie touched up the Measure 12 camouflage scheme, with drooping light and dark shades of gray and broad red stripes across the top of each gun turret so the ship was identifiable by American pilots as one of their own. The navy was very specific about camouflage; there was no room for a guy with a paintbrush to express himself creatively.

As the storm *Vincennes* weathered off the coast of South Africa on December 7 demonstrated, even steel ships need carpenters. Cabinets must be repaired, interior trim set in order. For this, *Vincennes'* carpenter shop was outfitted just like any land-bound shop: "Band saw, table saw, a planer," Ernie says. "I don't know why a planer, maybe hobby lobby for some officer." "Hobby lobby" is a phrase Ernie uses frequently. It's carpentry for fun.

A ship's carpenter has combat assignments as well: "He's a guy that plugs up the holes when it gets blasted," Ernie says.

Odd as it sounds, a mattress is an old solution to an even older problem: how to plug a rupture in a ship's hull. Mattresses were multipurpose tools to the navy. In *The Bluejacket's Manual*, the crews on damaged ships are advised to use them or kapok-filled life preservers to stanch the flow of water during battle: "In an emergency repair situation, do your best with what you have. If you are calm, alert, and work quickly with the tools you have, you can do much to keep the ship afloat and make her ready for action again."

"What else could you do?" Ernie says. "In a hurry like that? Stuff a mattress, brace it with a pole, and hope it works."

The poles, with a board nailed across one end in a T, were two-by-fours bracketed together so that the length of the pole quickly could be adjusted to fit the situation and keep the mattress nice and tight against unplanned structural events, like a torpedo hole in the hull. Ernie used poles rigged just like that years later on the job as a civilian carpenter. Not for torpedoes, but to hold sheetrock to the ceiling as he nailed it in place.

In wartime, it's a hit-or-miss strategy. A mattress shoved into the opening after a collision with another ship failed to keep the passenger steamer *Lady Elgin* from sinking in Lake Michigan in 1860, resulting in a huge loss of life. But the practice continued into World War II, with mattresses used to fill holes in the waterline of the carrier *Enterprise* after it was hit by torpedoes in August 1942 at the Battle of the Eastern Solomons. During the Battle of Leyte Gulf in 1944, *Claxton* used mattresses to shore up the nine-by-five-foot hole left at the waterline after the destroyer was struck by a kamikaze plane. Both ships survived.

And in case this hadn't occurred to new recruits unfamiliar with the physics of water and empty space, *The Bluejacket's Manual* also advises: "If flooding is not controlled, the ship will sink."

Carpentry and mattresses would not be of any value to *Vincennes* in the days ahead. In his search for adventure and whatever it was that he needed to get away from, Ernie was heading toward previously unheard-of destinations on the map: the Solomon Islands, Guadalcanal, and New Georgia Sound—and Savo Island.

On Father's Day in 2010, Ernie's family gave him a black leather-bound journal, urging him to record the memories he had of his ninety-three years. He began filling the pages with notes. Dates and friends' names came back to him, a flood of detail that included the jobs he'd held, his four marriages, the boats he'd built, trips to Europe, falling through the ice in a canal. Of *Vincennes*, he writes only thirteen words: "Spent time in the Pacific WW2. Lost a ship, ended in Maui, Hawaii."

EIGHT

Ernie and I had strolled purposefully through the decades during our first few interviews on the patio beneath the tulip tree. His grandparents, his parents, his first twenty-five years. Marriage, Pearl Harbor. We'd left *Vincennes* churning across the Pacific, with a date set for the following Monday to pick up the trail as he arrived at Guadalcanal and Savo Island, right where I wanted to be: the heart of the story. It had unfolded much more smoothly than expected.

The morning after our latest meeting, I received an email from Marilyn. In the subject line she'd written "Concern for Ernie." The message:

> Just wanted to let you know we will need to keep Ernie's sinking ship and rescue story out of the book. It seems that just talking about it has opened some very deep wounds and memories that have set off some nightmares keeping him awake at night. He said he did not want the name of the ship in as he did not want people to ask him about it as it brings up images that he had buried a long time ago. He said it wakes him up and he can still hear some of the guys crying out in the water and images that he cannot face even today. So I guess we need to be honor that part of his story and tell all about the interesting stories he had other times and in Maui where he had some funny stories to share. He does have enough to share without details of that horrible day. Thanks for honoring this request.

In the short time that I'd known Marilyn, she seemed to be the kind of person who took care of business, leavened with occasional bouts of drama. Self-assured to the point of bluntness, although perhaps the kind of personality that's needed to shepherd a busload of American senior citizens around Europe. Here, the message was clear enough: Ernie's nightmares had returned. I suspected they'd never completely gone away. He couldn't erase the memory of his fellow sailors screaming for help in the burning water. Undiagnosed post-traumatic stress disorder, I suspected. Or, more likely, unacknowledged post-traumatic stress disorder. That seemed to be how a lot of the old veterans—and the leaders who sent them to war—dealt with the problem. Ignore it and get on with your life. As for the soldiers, sailors, and airmen who couldn't shake it, the young men and women who found the horror too profound so that it suffocated what should have been long, healthy, productive lives? Well, that was a cost of war that no one bothered to calculate.

Reading the email, I was stunned, guilt ridden, and uncertain as to what to do next. I had played the lead role in reawakening this long-sleeping monster within an old veteran who should be left to enjoy his final years in peace.

I was also disappointed.

A few days later, I cautiously sent an email to Julie, Ernie's step-daughter, laying out the value of resuming work on the book, the tale of this self-made carpenter who rebuilt his life over and over and over. And we needed the story of what happened on *Vincennes* as well. In all honesty, I wrote to her, I couldn't see writing a man's life story and leave out the most dramatic part.

She let Ernie's nightmares and Marilyn's concerns settle for a few days, then talked it over with them. They agreed to proceed with one caveat: we were not to discuss the battle. I would be left to my own devices as to how to present the sinking of *Vincennes* to the reader. Perhaps sift through the existing resources about that muggy and extraordinarily dark evening that smothered the southwestern Pacific Solomons.

This approach was actually a relief to me. I didn't want to be the guy who ruined the private truce between war and peace that this sturdy veteran had worked out on his own.

"I'm meeting with him tomorrow morning," I wrote to Julie, "and if he brings it up and tells me again that he doesn't want to address the subject, I may talk with him in vague terms about his place in history. But I'm not pushing him on it."

* * *

It was raining that next Monday morning. Ernie and I sat at the kitchen table. Marilyn wasn't home; it was very quiet in the room. The only sound was a clock ticking and an occasional sigh from the aging refrigerator as its electric motor switched off. Ernie apologized for not being able to bring himself to talk about the battle. He stared at me with big eyes behind his eyeglasses, eyes rimmed red with age. I told him I understood. I explained how, as Marilyn had suggested, I would no longer be writing the book in chronological order but in chapters covering the different aspects of his life. Carpentry, the marriages, even his funny stories from Maui.

"Sort of episodic?" Ernie said.

Yeah. Episodic. Ernie frequently surprised me like that. A carpenter who understood the construction options of a nonfiction book. Must have picked it up on a TV talk show sometime.

We spent the morning talking about sailing. About Ernie's successes, his strategies. He warmed to the conversation. He was moving on.

But I guess he was moving on not far enough, not fast enough. The next morning, Julie forwarded another email from Marilyn. In the subject line Marilyn had written "No Go." The message:

> Ernie cannot handle any of the past regarding the Venesen ship. He is agitated about it and is having a hard time sleeping. It is not worth putting him through this in the book. So we will have to work around it and just mention his other parts of the navy. I want him to enjoy his meetings with Jeff and this has upset him too much. Sorry.

The Venesen ship. Marilyn sometimes had a casual relationship with spelling. But it was clear that Ernie was still struggling with his memories of the battle, despite neither of us bringing up *Vincennes*.

I'd put weeks of work into this project. I'd written a few chapters. I wanted to keep going, and not because I was already cashing checks from Julie, who was paying me for each chapter produced, but because I wanted to tell Ernie's story. All of it. It struck me as something valuable. We have enough books on how the great nineteenth-century industrial robber barons built this country. Enough analysis as to how many bodies should be laid at the feet of commanders such as Rear Admiral Victor Crutchley for the Savo Island disaster. We need all we can get about the roles, both small and large, played by guys like Ernie. How they made the twentieth century work. Their life ethic. I thought again of my late father-in-law. And how I would be poking around in his barn on that fifty acres of mid-Ohio farmland and find something like a hinge on a drawer that he'd made from a scrap of metal he'd found lying around. He didn't see the point of driving into town to buy a new hinge. I'd look around Ernie's house and see little details just like that.

* * *

Ernie was the oldest person I could remember ever meeting. My grandparents had seemed older, but when I did the math, I realized they were only in their fifties when I visited them as a little kid. My mom's parents lived in an apartment above a funeral home, which when I look back on it, now seems appropriate. I remember my mom telling me that my grandfather had been a talented artist as a young man and that he had fought with the American Expeditionary Forces in World War I and I should ask him about it.

He didn't look like an artist, just a ruined old man slumped on the couch in front of the television. I sometimes heard my mom and her sisters talking among themselves about how he'd drank too much when they were kids. If art had once been in his soul, it had long been drained away. Life, I suppose, will do that. But one afternoon during a break in the TV programming, I shyly asked him about the war. He didn't have much to say. That's when I began to understand that no, a lot of these guys didn't talk about it. And they didn't want to be asked.

* * *

I was sitting in a coffee shop with the novelist Joanna Scott. I don't want to give the impression that this is a frequent occurrence in my life. Talking to Pulitzer Prize–nominated writers, I mean. I sit in coffee shops all the time. Scott just happens to live in the same city as I do, and I was writing a profile on her, and she was telling me about writing her latest novel, *De Potter's Grand Tour*. Scott recalled how an old painting, a portrait of a man, had hung over the fireplace mantel, staring down at Scott since she was a little girl.

"I knew of him and knew he had disappeared at sea," she said. "It really haunted me."

The painting was of her great-grandfather, Armand de Potter. She'd spent five years digging into the documentation that remained of his life. In 1904 he had boarded the small passenger ship *Regele Carol* in Constantinople, bound for Greece. He never got off. No witnesses stepped forward to offer an explanation. Did de Potter commit suicide? Did he accidentally fall overboard? Was he murdered?

Scott didn't find enough. At least, not enough to solve the mystery. But that portrait became the inspiration for the novel.

"Yeah," I said. "I have one of those."

One of those family-tree mysteries. I visited my dad's mom often. Grandma Spevak had been a widow for decades, living with my unmarried aunt. They lived in several houses and condos over the years, but one constant was an oval-framed portrait in the family room, a sepia-tone artifact that takes you back to the turn of the last century. It was of a distant relative, a handsome guy in a military uniform who fought in World War I with the Austro-Hungarian Army. On the other side of the war from my mom's dad. That's how wars work. Two guys with probably the same simple desires in life, fighting for something larger that is ultimately of no consequence except to a few powerful people. Grandma Spevak said this forgotten relative had gone missing during the war. No one ever found out what had happened to him. Probably dead and buried in an unmarked grave with thousands of other young men who'd posed for portraits before going off to the war.

I was always fascinated that a man could just disappear like that.

Now Grandpa Valek was dead, taking whatever stories he had of World War I with him. Grandma Spevak was dead and with her went any remembrances of the hard romanticism of the early twentieth century. The details of their lives, even the big events, were missing. I'd allowed all of that to slip away.

* * *

A few days had passed, and Julie was again gently nudging Ernie back to the book. As 2010 drew to a close, Marilyn sent Julie an email:

> I read the chapter on the story of Ernie's ordeal, thinking how important it is to the book. Knowing how Ernie was feeling and feeling caught in the middle, I went to work today feeling sad and agreeing to what you said about your talk with Jeff. When I got home I was a bit quiet and feeling exhausted from work. Ernie says to me as I walk into the kitchen, "I decided to let them print the book as it was written. It has to be told even if it makes me sad. It is a part of my life and you can't choose parts of your life you don't want in a book about your life."

NINE

Ernie brings out a handful of photos and spreads them on the kitchen table. Here's a yellowed image of Ernie and a few teenage pals, including musketeer Paul Smith. It was taken during the Great Depression, and they'd driven to the East Coast after a hurricane had passed through, figuring on getting work with a landscaper. Lots of cleanup to be done. But the jobs didn't materialize, so here they were, laughing, relaxing on a New Jersey beach.

There is a similarly yellowed image of Ernie, Frank, and their mother. They're young men in their twenties. May looks young, too, but the cancer that will kill her probably already is spreading though her body.

Here's a fading color picture that looks to be from the late 1960s. It's Ernie's third wife, Evie, wearing some kind of creepy mask, sitting with a neighbor.

"He's long gone," Ernie says, a comment that accompanies most of the people in the old photographs.

Ernie's also in the photo, although you have to take his word for it. It's Halloween, and he's wearing a costume.

"I'd always wanted to be a gorilla," he says. "I jumped up on the bar at the Rochester Yacht Club, making a fool of myself, but the kids loved it."

Then he and Evie walked through their neighborhood, trick-or-treating for cocktails.

Here's a recent shot of Ernie's brother, Frank, on the sidewalk outside the apartment building where he lives in Florida, learning to use a walker. He'd started falling recently, and his son had insisted.

"I don't want to use a walker," Frank had grumped. "It makes me look old." He was ninety-eight.

And here's a photo of *Desire*, tied to a dock, eighty-five small pennants hanging from every available line. The poor boat looks like a flapper girl decked out in gold lamé. These were first-place flags won at races and regattas over the years. "I only keep the gold ones," Ernie says.

Sailing has been the consuming passion for this fellow with the oft-repeated mantra of "sailing is my life." The front room of his house, the remaining original thirty-two feet of shotgun shack that survived his remodeling, is nautical in nature. The narrowness of it, the wood ceiling beams, and the small windows suitable for rolling out muzzle-loading cannon have the feel of a space on one of Admiral Horatio Nelson's ships of the line. Although Nelson's ships wouldn't have likely had the cozy fireplace at the aft end, with slate on the floor apron cut and set in place by Ernie himself. The room opens into a kitchen and eating area as the updated aspects of the house begin to take over, accented with photos of *Desire* and rustic decorative signs proclaiming, "I'd rather be sailing." Some of the family is gathered beneath magnets on the refrigerator door, the rest of them crowd the walls alongside the stairs ascending to the second floor.

The newer section of the house—a family room that's now the first-floor bedroom, spare room, and stairway to the second floor—is where the true sailing shrine begins. Hallway shelves, end tables, and the broad top of the big television are lined with hardware that testifies to his skills. Silver bowls, brass sailboats, chrome balls, plaques, engraved beer mugs, plastic triangles representing mainsails, all from races of different lengths, on different bodies of water, sponsored by organizations such as the Oak Orchard Yacht Club, thirty-three miles up the east coast of Lake Ontario. Even awards for winning single-handed races. Ernie had rigged *Desire* so he could handle everything from the cockpit.

He has one trophy that he didn't win. Ernie's youngest girl, stepdaughter Julie, left it for him. "I took her out for a half hour so she could learn to sail," he says. "And the next day she won a race."

"I hope I don't win any more; I've got to clean 'em," Ernie adds, as he carefully makes his way back to the kitchen, wobbling a bit. After ninety-three years, it's the hardware he's collected in his joints that's acting up.

But the pursuit of the perfect sail was ongoing. Here's the latest trophy, sitting on the kitchen table: a small rectangle for a third-place finish two days earlier.

"There are two boats out there I absolutely can't beat," Ernie complains. "I'm sure their ratings are wrong."

They're Pearson 26s, naturally faster than his Columbia, which is a heavy three tons for twenty-six feet. The lighter Pearsons finished one and two. "They gave us time," Ernie says of the allowances that are supposed to ensure that these races are battles of sailors, not technology. "But not enough."

Another much longer race had been run the next day, the Hospice Regatta. But "I chose not to go this year because of the wind and the waves," he says.

"When I saw the water, I called the crew up, and they all thanked me. With a boat of my size, it's really tough on a crew to battle waves, high waves, a long distance, when the wind is blowing as strong as it is. I race for the enjoyment of being out there. When there's harsh conditions, I don't see any need for competing. I'm not that gung ho anymore. When it's a battle trying to stay upright, it's not fun anymore.

"I did win it one year," he says of the Hospice race, "but circumstances were different."

Different, indeed. Ernie's last few racing seasons had become a version of the old Cary Grant film *Operation Petticoat*. On the Tuesday-night Genesee Yacht Club series, he was sailing with a crew of four women who called themselves "Ernie's Angels": his stepdaughter Jan Ziobrowski, Mary Ann O'Leary, Mary Finnegan, and Jeanie Heil. For the Wednesday-evening Rochester Yacht Club races, Ernie and *Desire* were crewed by Jan Anderson, her husband John, and Craig Roth. Although they range in age from their forties to their sixties, Ernie calls them "my kids." The kids had been watching out for Dad the last couple of years while he recovered from a few surgeries, including a broken femur. His daughter Jan, he says, "treats me like a little kid. She's been wonderful the past two years while I've been incapacitated. All I had to do was steer and holler.

"One thing I've found out about women, they are very faithful. They don't call up at the last minute and cancel, like some guys do."

But the female crews, he admits, "have been a training program. Cranking the jib takes speed and strength," Ernie insists. "You really need a man on the come-abouts."

Racing in their later years, *Desire* and Ernie must rely on his guile.

"That's where my experience comes in," Ernie says.

Sailboat racing is strategy.

"You've gotta get a good start," Ernie says. "Cut it too cute, and you might end up crossing the starting line early and be forced to come around and try again. So already you're in last place. When the five-minute gun goes off, you have exactly five minutes to sail to where the starting line is. You have to maneuver around a lot of boats. Check out the other boats. Figure out which is the favorable end, because you want a starboard start. Hit starboard at the high point of the starting line. You could be on a port tack and another boat is on a starboard tack, and it looks like there's going to be a collision, so the starboard boat has the right of way."

This was once a matter of economics. Back to England and Ernie's grandparents and perhaps earlier, when Thames sailing barges loaded with cargo raced each other to the available dock space.

"The first boat in got the best prices," Ernie says.

Let the lawyers sort out the collisions. Yeah, it's always lawyers, even for those who seek the solace of water.

"You have to know the rules of the road," Ernie says. "There are sea lawyers out there. They win by fouling others up. They like to win by rules, not by skill."

Ernie recalls one such scourge with whom he had the misfortune to become entangled during a start.

"He cut in front of me; they call it barging. You're not supposed to do that. So I touched him. That's called a collision."

A gentle nudge, no damage done, but the sea lawyer went to the protest committee afterward. There wasn't much Ernie could say, since his sailing rage—just letting the guy know he was out of line—had happened right in front of the protest committee boat. Apparently barging is only a gentleman's agreement, whereas starboard's right of way is the law. Ernie was disqualified.

But sailing is not about the hot wind of postrace disputes. It's about the wind during the sail. Sailors use *sail* as a noun or a verb, the same way another man might announce he is going for a drive.

"You've gotta stay in clean wind," Ernie says.

"You don't sail behind a boat. . . . Stay out in the open. If there's a boat ahead of you, he's using up the air. If there's a boat ahead, it's all disturbed."

It is the rare sail in which the boat follows a constant compass line—in sailing it's called the rhumb line.

"I never go out to the rhumb line, because there might be a wind shift," Ernie says. "There are times when a rhumb line favors a boat—I would say 20 percent of the time—so you play the averages."

A large amount of data goes into Ernie's computing of those averages. He watched the weather reports, of course. But remember, Ernie came from an era before the Weather Channel, before local meteorologists bragging about the size of their Dopplers.

He watched the land. Factory and power station smokestacks in particular.

"If the smokestacks are blowing, I head to shore," Ernie says. "If the smokestacks are straight, I head out to sea, because the wind is out there."

He watched the clouds.

"It tells me if it's going to rain," Ernie says. "The clouds tell you what direction the upper wind is flowing. When you see clouds, there's usually wind. If they move steady, the surface wind is safe. If they start clearing out, the wind is going to die down."

He watched the water. In light winds, he would search for "cats' paws," ripples of action on the water, indicating that there's wind at the surface of an otherwise calm lake.

"A little burst here, a little burst there, and you look to see where they are," Ernie says. "Thirty seconds to a minute, then it's gone. There's a lot of luck in sailing in that kind of racing."

And he watched the other boats, before and between sails, when the winner is determined by the accumulated finishes over a series of races, as was the case with Ernie's most recent third-place finish. He'd studied "the leader, or who's closest to me." Only the fastest boat mattered. That's who he was racing.

"I ignore the other ones."

Ernie fetches another trophy, for his first-place finish in the 1985 Freedom Cup Race. It's a Plexiglas square with a clock mounted in it. Sailors respect barometers and clocks and things that measure. It's how they stayed safe—and navigated—for centuries. Sponsored by the Lake

Yacht Racing Association, the Freedom Cup was open to boats that were members of yacht clubs on Lake Ontario and Lake Erie. It was a long, overnight race, a real test of a sailor. This particular year, the course started out of Sodus Bay, east of Rochester, and headed east again to a buoy planted far out in the lake, then west to Rochester, and then back to Sodus Bay. Six divisions of boats, about ten in *Desire*'s class, each division starting ten minutes apart.

"I hugged the shore, the rest of the fleet went out to sea," following the rhumb line, Ernie says. "There was a heck of a current that year."

A current that usually runs west to the east from the Niagara River, curling inward on itself to the east before moving on to the St. Lawrence Seaway around Oswego. But this season, the powerful current had left the usual eddy farther west, off Sodus Point, so boats sprinting from the starting line and heading out into the lake were battling that current. Plus, "The shoreline creates friction and little pockets of wind," Ernie says. Running along the coast at an angle slightly perpendicular to the other boats, he was seeking wind—and finding it—as the other boats drifted with slack sails. By the time Ernie turned *Desire* up into the lake, he'd taken the longer route east but had made much better time.

Now, heading toward the marker set about a mile out into the lake, Ernie could see the other sails far to port, particularly the three fastest boats working upwind. He could also see that their progress was slow. So rather than tacking toward the buoy, he held his course, hoping to get lucky and catch some fresh, clean air.

"The wind doesn't completely die out there," he says. "There's always a couple of wind changes."

By keeping his boat on the move, Ernie put himself in position to find those changes. Finally tacking toward the marker, he caught a breeze and rounded his way toward Rochester with good wind and the current pushing him. The other boats were still straining for the buoy, looking for a breath to fill their sails. But the wind filled Ernie's spinnaker, the sail at the foremast, the one that picks up the boat and really pushes it after the mainsail has done the heavy lifting.

"That was the most perfect spinnaker race I ever had," Ernie says of the dash back to the coast.

Now, far out in front, it was getting late. The thoughtful quiet of a boat under full sail settled around *Desire*. Collecting gold pennants makes for a good picture, but . . .

"I saw the sun set," Ernie says. A larger picture emerges, feeding the romantic soul of men like Ernie.

"I saw the moon come up." He was gliding back along the coast, heading toward Sodus Bay with *Desire*, all alone in the darkness, beneath the stars.

"I saw the moon disappear."

His three crewmen had crawled into the bunks, and Ernie handled the boat by himself.

"I saw the sun rise."

TEN

Perhaps an aging sailor always can enjoy a good sunrise because they looked the same back in 1931, a time when he camped out in swamps and along canals, drifting in canoes alongside barges manned by sweating men doing men's work. The stuff of adventure for a fifteen-year-old boy.

Just before he was to start high school, Ernie, his brother, and two friends set off on such an adventure, Ernie and Frank in one canoe, Donald and Morris in a second, paddling off one morning from the Pittsford canal launch, following the canal south into the Montezuma Marshes. These had been largely drained by the construction of the Cayuga-Seneca Canal, although the water had been restored and the area became a wildlife refuge a few years after Ernie and his entourage passed through.

But even before that, "Migratory birds would really load it up," Ernie recalls. The canoeists watched an eclipse of the sun, then glided to Cayuga Lake, the Seneca River, and Seneca Lake, portaging their canoes around canal locks, enjoying having much of this to themselves. Tugs cajoled barge loads of oil and grain along the canals. Sometimes it would be a string of six barges, each barge seventy feet in length, an ungainly water train so long that the last barge was for the crew to live aboard.

"When they were moving, they used to churn the bottom up because they were so close to the bottom of the canal," Ernie remembers.

The two canoes tied up to the tail end of one of these convoys for a night ride on the way back, even passing through the locks with the barges, sometimes stopping long enough for the boys to gather a dinner of fruit from the trees and corn from the fields.

They were gone for two weeks, and Ernie was a couple of days late starting high school. But he would do that: shrug his shoulders at the rules now and then.

Miss school a few days? "Sure, why not?"

Go AWOL from the navy? "Sure, why not?"

Ernie and I had leapfrogged Savo Island to his final twenty-two months of service during World War II on the Hawaiian island of Maui. Now he was telling stories, one episode after another, of pushing the authoritarian envelope. Something about these tales didn't sound at all like "the navy way" that he'd been taught at Great Lakes Naval Station. At Naval Air Station, Kahului, Carpenter's Mate Second Class Ernie Coleman was assigned to the carpenter's shop, with duties that included tending to public works projects on the island. The combat zones were far over the horizon, so after Savo Island, this was welcome R&R. Rest and recuperation. The duties included merely "setting up the beer tent," Ernie says, "building shelves and iceboxes where they stored the beer and so forth for dispensing. We put up a couple of small buildings. I learned what a two-by-four was for, and what a two-by-ten was for."

Ernie and his fellow navy carpenters were set up in a warehouse, "open twenty-four hours," he says, "equipped with a stove, stuff like that. Anyone had a problem, they could call us." He started specializing in building shipping boxes. Easy-to-handle, quarter-inch plywood crates held together with big screws, so a serviceman could fit a dime edge into the screwhead and easily open the box.

"I could knock out one in fifteen minutes," Ernie says. Soon enough they had a little operation set up as well, with Ernie trading the boxes for food, particularly baked goods. Small things that made war a little easier. Someone even traded Ernie's services for a 1928 Dodge Victory Six with a starter-generator crank in the front. The only money he ever had to spend on it was for gas, oil, and a $1.21 headlight bulb. That's where Ernie told me about replacing the exhaust system with the steel exhaust pipe from a warplane and making a muffler with a shell casing from a five-inch naval gun. Like I said, these guys had the self-contained, entre-preneurial savvy that leaves the generations to follow shaking our heads in amusement—and admiration. Ernie and his fellow carpenters had fash-ioned a minor pirate kingdom on the edge of the Pacific war. Kind of like

McHale's Navy, the TV show from the 1960s built around the crew of a PT boat, a patrol torpedo boat. Scam artists who just wanted to slide through the war as comfortably as possible. I could see Ernie as the Ernest Borgnine character, bartering his way into a little empire of ease.

"All because I made these shipping boxes in my line of duty," Ernie says.

* * *

The winter Kona winds sweeping through the islands, bringing their big rainstorms with them, weren't much of a disruption to Maui's unrelentingly fine weather. Boring, Ernie has said. Ernie was easily bored. He built himself a surfboard and paddled out into the waves.

"There wasn't a lot of surf," he says, but he'd built a window in the board so at least he could look down into the water.

Possibilities began emerging when Ernie got back into the pleasure craft shipwright business again.

"I must have been talking to one of the guys about building my Snipe," he says of the day his division officer stopped by looking for a favor. "He loved to sail, but he didn't know how to build a boat." Ernie went to work. Orders are a part of the navy way.

"We had a pretty good-size lumberyard there," he says, and had soon fashioned a sixteen-foot dinghy out of white pine, since mahogany wasn't readily available.

That boat wasn't quite big enough for the division officer, so Ernie went to work again, starting with a twenty-foot lifeboat slightly wider than the dinghy. He mounted a mast on it and added a stainless-steel centerboard, since lifeboats don't have the keel necessary for sailing. Cotton for the sail was tough to come by.

"A buddy of the lieutenant at the airfield got me nylon for the sail," Ernie says. A parachute, actually. "I think I was a pioneer for nylon sails." At war's end, "When I came back, no more cotton sails. They're harder to maintain. Cotton sails need to be dried before you put them away."

This boat was to the division officer's satisfaction, and Ernie used it four or five times himself. A fine diversion for the officers, the boat also proved to be an excellent turtle-hunting craft. Ernie worked at the shop with a couple of Hawaiians—both immigrants, a German and an Irishman—who knew their way through turtle territory. With the boat under sail, they'd quietly move into the middle of a group of turtles. Someone would slip into the water and grab on to one.

"The turtle wants to go down," Ernie says. "When a turtle's working, it sticks its neck out. The guy takes his knife out"—Ernie makes a slashing motion with an imaginary knife—"it's dead right there."

They collected seven or eight turtles during the raid, some weighing one hundred pounds, and dropped them off at the Seabees base next door to the naval air station. Ernie was invited to a turtle dinner the next night.

"Eleven kinds of meat," he says; turtle meat, prepared eleven different ways. "I had the turtle soup. It was very good. Tasted like chicken."

His carpentry skills paid off with other adventures, as Ernie began sampling the American military arsenal. Someone offered him a submarine trip.

"Why not?" Ernie says. "Well, talk about a boring ride. You climb down in a hole, sit there, feel some tilting. Anyone who was claustrophobic would go ape."

The PT boat was more his speed.

"For some reason, they wouldn't tell you how fast we were going," Ernie says. That was probably classified information, so that the Japanese couldn't calculate the boats' movements.

"I figured at least sixty."

Ernie found out later that sixty-five miles per hour was more like it.

"It had five engines hooked to one screw," he says. "Lots of power there."

"And I learned one thing," Ernie adds. When they hit swells, "The chief said, 'Whatever you do, don't stand flat-footed. Bend your knees.'" Until his final sailing days, that was still how Ernie stood on a boat when it was bounding over the waves.

Hitchhiking a ride on a Curtiss SB2C Helldiver was another unauthorized adventure.

"Take my place," a Helldiver tail gunner suggested to Ernie one day. "We're just going up for maneuvers."

"Sure," Ernie said. "Why not?"

Maybe not because that SB2C designation meant, to the pilots, "son of a bitch second class," due to the plane's beastly handling qualities. A two-man crew operated the Helldiver, with the pilot up front and the tail gunner a good bit behind him in a separate cockpit facing the rear, making it easy enough for Ernie to take the real gunner's place without drawing attention. All Ernie had to do was sit in the back and watch as the pilot and the rest of the squadron hit a one-hundred-foot island with tiny practice torpedoes.

"I never realized g-forces were that strong," Ernie says.

"At four Gs, your mouth is open—you can't close it—every part of your body is pushing back in the seat."

At twenty-seven thousand feet, the pilot radioed back to Ernie, "There's our landing."

Ernie looked down. It was an aircraft carrier.

"I thought, 'Oh, no, we're not gonna land on that little thing?'"

Oh, yes. Having descended and now scooting along fifty to sixty feet above the waves, "the carrier is higher than we are," Ernie says. "The next time I looked, there wasn't any carrier." It had descended into the trough of a wave. Ernie remembers thinking "I just hope this guy knows how to land this thing."

He did, the hook at the tail end of the Helldiver snagging the arresting cable.

"It snaps you pretty good," Ernie says. "I had a shoulder strap on, but I almost hit the cowling." They crawled out of the plane and the pilot looked at Ernie and asked, "Where's Roy?"

"He asked me to take his place."

"Are you a tail gunner?"

"I'm a carpenter's mate."

The pilot shook his head and walked away.

Mere shenanigans in comparison to the weekend that Ernie went AWOL. Absent without leave.

It started innocently enough.

"A couple of buddies in the barracks," Ernie says, talking about home and wives and girlfriends, and suddenly Ernie was issued a dare: bet you can't get home to see Ruth. Once again, for Ernie this was a question of, "Why not?"

"One thing led to another, and all of a sudden I'm on a plane."

Anyone bumming a ride in the naval air force needed his own parachute.

"You'd better bring it back," his tail gunner buddy said, handing over the chute. Ernie caught a ride to Hickham Field, then talked his way onto a two-engine light bomber, the A-20 Havoc. It's the version outfitted with a Plexiglas nose where the bombardier sat. Since no bombing opportunities would present themselves on this flight, that was Ernie's seat.

"Kind of like flying in a patio," he says.

Ernie enjoyed a fine view on the ride to San Diego, then cross-country to the Tonawanda airport outside of Buffalo, before taking the bus to Rochester, arriving early Saturday evening.

"What'd you do, get kicked out of the service?" said a shocked Ruth.

"No, just stopping for a visit."

The next morning, Ruth drove him back to the airport.

"I caught the same plane back that I came over with," Ernie says. "Nobody knew I was gone." The tail gunner got his parachute back, unused.

"It was a stupid thing to do," Ernie says. "If I had gotten stranded, they would have put me in the brig for the rest of the war."

ELEVEN

If Ernie truly was a regular guy often caught up in remarkable circumstances, I needed an appropriate literary model. I began to think of him as a character in a John Prine song. Prine's men and women do the best they can in a world that can be unforgiving to the little guy. They dream of making love to someone they don't know. They put up with the small dramas of disagreeable relatives. They fall in love, settle in with someone for life, and try to save a marriage, all while standing by peaceful waters. They grow old. They reminisce, resigned to dealing with memories both amusing and painful. Sometimes they go to war. Sam Stone did. He's one of Prine's most memorable characters, the one who returned from the Vietnam War with "the hole in his arm where all the money goes." Heroin.

All of them everyday uncelebrated heroes.

* * *

Grandma Spevak, whom I mentioned earlier, led one of those lives of storybook poverty. There was a photo of her as a young girl, cutting the heads off chickens for the family dinner. That sounds like a Prine song. She had to pluck the chickens after the beheadings, rough work for a kid. Maybe that's why she always brought a bucket of Kentucky Fried Chicken to family gatherings. It was just a lot easier.

Like Ernie's family, my family was immigrants. Most Americans are—we tend to forget that once we're established. That migration to America is really the only interesting story in my family. We weren't explorers or criminals or war heroes. Just people doing the best they could, and no better. As best I remember it, this is the story told by Grandma Spevak.

Europe was on the edge of war and much of her family was migrating to America in the early part of the century. A great-grandfather of mine, whom I never knew, was already there and sent for the rest of his family. They left Austria-Hungary and traveled east to meet the ship that was to take them to America. I don't know if the port was Southampton, England, from where the ship sailed, or Cherbourg, France, where it stopped briefly, but the family didn't have enough money to book passage. It sailed without them, and they returned home. Happily so, I remember my grandmother saying. Many of the family members hadn't wanted to leave Austria-Hungary for America anyway.

But I guess my great-grandfather had made up his mind that America was the family's future. A year later, they'd put together enough money to come to America on SS *George Washington*. They were poor immigrants who could only afford space in steerage, in the depths of the ship. But my grandmother, Anna, a little girl at the time, remembers coming out on deck to play. She tripped and fell, cutting herself, and a rich woman used her silk handkerchief to stop the bleeding. When Anna had returned belowdecks, her mother—my great-grandmother, another relative I never knew—had her daughter wash the blood from the handkerchief, return topside, find the rich woman, and return the handkerchief.

George Washington arrived at New York City, discharging its rich passengers at the wharf while the immigrants were shuttled off to Ellis Island. My ancestors continued the journey to the Cleveland suburb of Bedford, Ohio, because that's where so many of their relatives and fellow countrymen had settled.

And that ship that they couldn't afford to board a year earlier? News reports being intermittent and illiteracy so prevalent, they didn't even hear of what had happened to RMS *Titanic* until they arrived in America.

I imagine that story is one powerful explanation for why I've always been interested in big ships and the tragedies that sometimes surround them. When you're a kid, catastrophe is a romantic notion. As an elementary school student, I sketched pictures of sunken ships. Some years ago at my parents' house, I came across a drawing done by my brother and me. It was a simple crayon seascape of clouds, ocean waves, and nothing else. It was entitled "At the Titanic."

* * *

It wasn't long into our relationship that I had reasons to visit Ernie beyond the weekly Monday-morning sessions. Ernie and Marilyn invited my wife and me over one evening for a glass of wine. The women were drinking white; Ernie and I were drinking red. It wasn't an interview; I didn't take notes. We talked about places we'd been. Soon the glass of wine became a second then a third. Ernie fetched two more bottles, another white, another red. As the wine in our glasses dropped, Ernie filled them again, his included. It was as though he was afraid that we'd notice our glasses were empty and interpret it as a sign that the evening was over, and he didn't want it to end.

* * *

As I began filling in the details of Ernie's life, the complexities became easier to see. A John Prine tune wasn't enough. The literary model began to take on grander themes. In my eyes, Ernie emerged as a character from a Haruki Murakami novel: an old man with a harrowing backstory. There are a few of those in Murakami's writing, like Mr. Honda in *The Wind-Up Bird Chronicle*. The aging fortune-teller who utters philosophical vagueness such as, "You go up when you're supposed to go up and down when you're supposed to go down." He's an old man who tells stories of the 1939 battle of Nomonhan, on the border of Outer Mongolia and Manchuria, where Mongolian and Soviet forces caught without food, water, and bullets faced Japanese troops, resorting to desperately throwing Molotov cocktails.

The differences being that Ernie didn't deal in philosophical vagueness. He spoke in practicalities like, "If the smokestacks are blowing, I head to shore."

And he still didn't talk about the war.

TWELVE

You join the Navy to see the world, they say. But they don't give you a guidebook.

With the Japanese surrender in 1945, Carpenter's Mate Second Class Ernie Coleman left the navy as what was called an inactive reserve, which meant he could be called back to duty in the event of some crisis. How long could the planet go without a problem? Long enough to excuse Ernie from the next one?

Five years. Not long enough. In summer 1950, North Korea invaded South Korea. By spring 1951, Ernie was back right where he didn't want to be. The navy, housed in Flushing Barracks at the Brooklyn Navy Yard. Where experience was a plus. He was thirty-five years old, but that was kid stuff. "There was a guy that was seventy-two, called in as a reserve," Ernie says. "Seventy-two years old, and they expect him to go out to sea?"

Maybe if the navy was recommissioning Old Ironsides. Still, many of the routines hadn't changed from Ernie's last stretch in the service. If his name wasn't on an assignment roster at 8 a.m. each morning, by 8:01 a.m. he and his barracks mates had all of New York City waiting for them. Very quickly, these eager new sailors discovered that you can get something for free, at least as an introductory offer. Heroin. Word spread through the barracks that a free high could be had by servicemen, perhaps as a patriotic gesture.

"You tell the guy, 'Joe sent me,'" Ernie says. "I went with two other guys. I figured, what the hell, why not? I just wondered what the experience was. So he just gives you a shot in the arm"—Ernie simulates a hypodermic going into the veins at the crook of his elbow—"and now I'm a prospective customer."

Turned loose on the streets of New York City with the first-time rush of heroin, the sailors roared through the Fifth Avenue bars, having a big time.

"Someone said, 'boo,' everybody laughed," Ernie says. "We were in one bar acting so happy, they threw us out.

"That next morning, I woke up with a hangover and a half. Now the trick is, you have to go back and get another fix."

Despite his limited experience with narcotics, Ernie knew the next one wouldn't be free. He dealt with his post-party withdrawal on his own.

"It showed me something," he says. "Drugs are not fun."

And soon enough came the distraction of his 8 a.m. assignment: Norfolk Naval Base in Norfolk, Virginia, to work in the carpentry shop on a training AKA. The attack cargo ship, as these 450-foot holdovers from World War II were known, was designed to efficiently load and unload military cargo at a beachhead. Attack cargo ships also transported and launched LCMs, landing craft mechanized, generally fifty-six feet long, shallow-draft barges designed for landing vehicles on a beach. And LCVPs, landing craft, vehicle, personnel, better known as the famous Higgins Boat, twenty feet shorter than an LCM. Turned loose from the attack cargo ships moored offshore in relative safety, the Higgins Boats crashed onto the beach, the ramp dropped down into the surf and sand, and troops charged out into a hail of machine-gun fire and exploding mortar shells. These landing crafts were a common sight at the D-Day landings at Normandy Beach, islands throughout the Pacific during World War II, and in a handful of films featuring John Wayne.

And that was the problem on one fatal afternoon that Ernie recalls during training exercises while anchored about three miles off Morehead City, North Carolina, a deepwater port with facilities for landing craft. Like the AKAs, the largely plywood Higgins Boats were relics from the war that had ended five years earlier. Ernie's ship dropped one in the water, and the soldiers scrambled down the netting on the side of the ship into the landing craft.

"The bow logs had rotted," Ernie recalls, "the hinges fell off and the thing went down."

As he remembered it, only two men were pulled alive from the water. Twenty men in fully loaded packs drowned.

In the second-guessing that followed the tragedy, "Word got around that I knew something about carpentry and boats," Ernie says. He was put in charge of the crew that inspected the remainder of the landing craft. He found two or three more with rotted bow logs.

Ernie's expertise in repairing these antiquities was greeted with enthusiasm by the ship's captain, who promptly instructed Ernie that his two grandkids back home needed twin beds. Ernie fashioned them in the ship's carpentry shop and was rewarded with a box of Cuban cigars.

"And I didn't even smoke," Ernie says.

If heroin didn't give him pause, certainly smoking in 1951 wouldn't be an issue. Ernie joined the smokers hanging out on the ship's fantail one evening. He borrowed a menthol cigarette from a sailor, "took a puff and started to cough," Ernie says.

"The guy says, 'That's not the way to start. Take small puffs.'"

The first one was free, but it remained a cheap vice. "Cigarettes were five cents a pack then," Ernie says. "I got hooked."

* * *

Before leaving Rochester for that second stint with the navy, he'd gotten hooked in another manner of speaking as well. Ernie met Jen Beachner at the Newport Yacht Club's 1948 Turkey Fest. As a teenager, the third of nine girls growing up in Rochester, she had been the 1931 Lilac Festival queen.

"She was a good dancer, and I loved to dance," Ernie says. "Ruth was not a good dancer. So I got to know her well through dancing. She was a very friendly, outgoing person." Jen's husband was a bartender at the club, and when Ernie would go to the bar for drinks, he'd ask, "Is Jen having a good time?"

"I guess so," Ernie would say.

He knew so. "We cheated a couple of times; let's put it that way," Ernie admits. "We had a lot of discussions about a lot of things. She would always listen, whereas Ruth never did. She always had a word in edgewise."

They went out together as couples, but when Ernie and Jen were alone together, they commiserated about their marriages.

"He was a good guy," Ernie says of Jen's husband, a crewman himself on a larger sailboat. "And he was very dull."

And Ernie, with the sheen of a newly returned World War II Navy veteran, had some status.

"I was the top sailor at the club," he says. "Everyone wanted to know what I did and learn what I did."

Ernie and Ruth had bought a house on Titus Avenue, a rural stretch of road not far from the two most important places to Ernie: Lake Ontario and Irondequoit Bay. The couple was at the center of the Newport Yacht Club social circle. Yachting strangers they'd met in the afternoon were throwing their sleeping bags on the floor that night.

"We had a ball," Ernie says. He was also building another Snipe—perhaps with the usual goal of manufacturing an excuse to get away from Ruth—while remaining mindful of one basic principle of building a boat in the basement. Even when the basement has a large, exterior walk-in door: "Can I get the boat out without tearing the place apart?" Ernie says. "This happened to one of my buddies. He had to tear apart the foundation to get the boat out."

The Snipe was a beauty, but the distraction it offered didn't save the marriage. Before Ernie was recalled into the service, he'd asked Ruth for a divorce and handed over to her the house and the car.

"I left with my tools and my clothes," Ernie says. And he left with one concession from Ruth. The Snipe, waiting in the basement, was about three-fourths finished.

"She allowed me to finish the boat," Ernie says.

* * *

Ernie calls Jen "the love of my life." Divorce—hers as well, now—cleared the way for that story to continue. With Ernie assigned to Norfolk, Jen soon followed, renting an apartment and finding a job as a secretary at a furniture company.

"If we had maneuvers, I'd be gone for a couple of days," he says. Otherwise, the Korean War was banking hours for Ernie.

As his year's commitment, already extended to eighteen months, drew to a close, "The Korean War was getting pretty critical at the time," Ernie says. The fall of 1952 came down to the Battle of Triangle Hill, the bloodiest engagement of the year, setting the conflict on a course of eternal stalemate. Ernie's training ship was sent to the Mediterranean to be closer to the action, but it went without Ernie, who spent his last month of service as a watchman on another AKA quietly docked at Norfolk before he was sent home. He and Jen returned as a married couple, having driven to Elizabeth City, North Carolina, on a one-day liberty briefly spent with a justice of the peace.

"To make it legal, so to speak," Ernie says. "In those days, people didn't approve of people living together."

Arriving home around Christmastime, their life together in Rochester started with a week living with one of Jen's sisters before they found an apartment on Monroe Avenue, one of the main retail drags in the city. Ernie immediately began working as a carpenter until the union went on strike. He quit and began working on his own. Remodeling jobs, building new homes.

"Just making money to survive, enjoying what I'm doing," he says. Survival, because unemployed was no way for a newly married man to build a life. Enjoyment, because building things is a sense of accomplishment that can be measured.

"When a pile of lumber is delivered, and you see an empty basement and all that, and ultimately turn it into a house," Ernie says, "it's a nice, creative feeling."

He didn't get that same creative feeling at places where he felt "cooped up," as he liked to say. Like Gleason Works. Or a later job at the General Motors parts manufacturing plant on Lexington Avenue. Moves responding to that need for money to survive and his own restlessness. But again, not satisfying. Watching one machine fold a piece of metal into a tube, a second machine seal the fold and a third machine cut it off to the proper length—there, you have a gas line—is not the sort of work for a man whose mind drifts to thoughts of sails filling with air.

No, he was better suited to carpentry. Working on boats at the yacht club, refinishing wood fittings, the kind of thing he still was doing at age ninety-three. Jen took another job as a secretary, and they found a cottage to rent on Harrison Terrace in Summerville on the Lake Ontario shore. Over the years, Ernie had been adding skills to his carpenter's bag: plumbing, laying tile, cabinetmaking, heating. The cottage sat on a large lot, and he not only remodeled it into a year-round residence, but he helped build a home on the lot for his new landlords, Jake and Eileen.

"I got to be pretty good friends with Jake," Ernie says.

One thing the carpenter hadn't gotten around to building was a family. But when the opportunity presented itself, in 1956, Ernie and Jen became forty-year-old parents. The baby was two days old when they picked her up, adopted straight from the hospital. The mother was a friend of a friend, the baby from an adulterous relationship. The transaction was discreet and simple. They named her Patricia, and Jen quit work to take care of her.

* * *

Ernie was forced to rebuild his life repeatedly over his nine-plus decades in small and large ways. Moving from job to job was a small way. Divorcing Ruth was a big one. Taken separately, each was a life experience, and all too often they were not pleasant moments. A test of the will. In the metaphor of each of life's experiences being a separate thread, Ernie was about to weave another one into the rope.

Pat—Ernie called her Tricia, sometimes Patti—was four years old in 1960, almost ready for school. Ernie and Jen had gone to bed, but he awoke in the middle of the night, sensing something wrong. He looked over at the twin bed next to him. Jen wasn't there.

"I just felt something happened," Ernie says. He got up and walked through the house and came across a spouse's worst fear: Jen was lying on the living room floor.

"I looked her over; she wasn't there," he says. "I popped on some clothes, ran next door, and started hammering on the door, 'Jake, Jen is out, I think she's dead.'"

An ambulance was called, but Jen couldn't be revived. Ernie didn't know what it was then, but he knew now: a party, too many drinks, and asphyxiation due to choking to death on her own vomit. The body doesn't respond properly to an emergency. Perhaps as a way to make such a death a little more understandable, a little easier to accept, when telling this story, Ernie adds as an aside that bandleader Tommy Dorsey also died in this manner.

"It's one of those freaky things," he says.

Jimi Hendrix, too, I tell Ernie. I'm not sure Ernie was familiar with Hendrix.

"I was devastated," Ernie says. "People said, 'Are you still going to keep Patti?' 'Certainly I am. I'm her father as far as I'm concerned.'"

He lost himself in work. But the hours spent in garages and basements in search of solace while building boats wasn't the true Ernie. He feared being alone.

"I don't like myself that much," Ernie says. "In fact, I don't like to go sailing alone. I crave friends."

Yacht club friends helped out. Jake and Eileen next door helped out. Eileen watched Pat while Ernie was at work and cooked dinners for them, as did a divorced neighbor with two kids.

Eileen, it also must be noted now, had an identical twin sister, Evie.

Evie and her husband Gilbert Ross had been a part of Ernie and Jen's social circle, along with Jake and Eileen. The Newport Yacht Club was one setting, movies another, downtown bars yet one more. Jake was in the meat business, so the group also circulated among the restaurants and bars where he sold prepared hamburger patties and chicken cutlets.

"We did a lot of drinking in those days," Ernie says.

And Gilbert was the kind of guy who would walk into a bar and offer to buy drinks for everyone. That caught up with him. Deeply in debt, deeply depressed, one day he walked into the woods behind his Spencerport house and took his own life.

He left behind a wife and five kids. The oldest child, Judy, was already married and on her own, but Shirley, Charlie, John, and Janice were still at home with Evie. Jan was only a few months older than Pat.

"Jen would send baskets of food to Evie," Ernie says. On some weekends, Evie would bring the kids to her sister's house to enjoy the lake.

Maybe, in their tight social circle, they all saw this coming. A couple of years after Evie was widowed, just a few months after Jen had died, "I started dating Evie," Ernie says. "Eileen would babysit Tricia. We hit it off very well. She was a wonderful dancer and I loved to dance."

He was dancing again, just as he had with Jen. Within the year, Ernie and Evie married. As with Jen, a justice of the peace handled the paperwork. Ernie was never big on ceremony or lavish events. They moved into Evie's home, an interesting structure for a fellow in the carpentry trade, particularly one who had built a sailboat from a kit: it was a Bennett kit home, similar to the more familiar prefab Sears catalog homes. Houses delivered as piles of lumber, arriving at a hole in the ground. A home in the early stages of its life, just as Ernie was accustomed to seeing, except the pieces were precut and numbered.

The railroad tracks were nearby. Probably the same tracks that the house had arrived on. That was an annoyance. But soon enough, a guy gets used to the racket.

"When a train slowed down, everyone woke up," Ernie says. "At night, you never heard them when they were roaring through."

Pat's adjustment was a concern.

"When I was alone with her, I pretty much spoiled her," Ernie says.

That's if spoiling her was taking his daughter sledding at Durand-Eastman Park, just a short distance from their home on Harrison Terrace, and teaching her how to ride a bike, playing catch, and going to the zoo that was once tucked in among the trees of Durand-Eastman. Sounds like normal activities. But after the two of them had moved from the idyllic Summerville cottage, Ernie saw that their new home was on a busy road and nervously got rid of the bike.

And Pat, who had once been the center of attention, "was no longer the kingpin," Ernie admits. "She made up for it by being around a big family."

Six kids. Ernie loved it. He even drew on his old high school baseball skills as a backyard catcher for Charlie, a youth league pitcher.

Ernie was building a new life, but almost without being aware of it at first, he began rebuilding his old life as well. Life on Harrison Terrace with Jen had left him with a longing for the Lake Ontario breezes of Summerville. He felt comfortable there. When a summer cottage at 9 Madison Terrace became available in 1963, just a few streets over from Harrison Terrace, Ernie and Evie bought it and began converting it into a year-round residence.

Two years later, they bought another one just yards away, a few houses from where Madison dead-ended at the beach. Working in his spare time, mostly on weekends, it took Ernie seven years to renovate it to his liking.

"How much can you do in one afternoon?" he asks, as though he feels as if he has to apologize for taking so long.

Enough, given enough afternoons. He expanded on the house's basic, seventy-two-foot-long shotgun-shack design, knocking off forty feet of it and putting a two-story addition on the back. This was where he and Evie would live out their lives. The little patio table at the side of the house, beneath the shade of the impressively tall tulip tree next to the white hydrangeas, was where he sat in the summer of 2010. A ninety-three-year-old man telling these stories at the house on Madison Terrace, where he could look out the little window and see the lake. You can't see the world from there. But you can see the piece of the world that made sense to Ernie.

THIRTEEN

Ernie's man cave was beneath the Madison Terrace house. A small basement partitioned into three rooms, although it's hard to tell with all the lumber leaning this way and that, like sailors still in search of their land legs. But the shop begins to make sense as you poke about in the dingy, worn light. Details emerge. Over there, ropes for *Desire*, looped and knotted in nautical ways. Here, a drill press. Table saw. Band saw. Vises. Dust. Wood trim, with a loop of twine at each end, hangs from the ceiling. Shelves overloaded with cans of paint and solvents; who knows how old some of that stuff is? Ernie nailed the tin lids from baby-food jars into the wood floor joists overhead. He filled the jars with screws and nails, then twisted the jars back into their lids, where they hang like bats. This shop was the sum of little tricks that Ernie picked up from the carpenter shops that he had been in throughout the years.

"Here's a project I'm working on for a client," Ernie says, holding up a child's tiny rocking chair. It looks like an antique. It's old, anyway. Ernie would make sure the joints fit nice and tight, then sand, stain, and varnish whenever he got around to it. Seeing some of the other projects pushed into the shop's corners, you get the feeling that the kid for whom that renovated chair was intended was probably too big to fit in it now.

Ernie appreciates the final result of his labors. But he is more enamored of the process.

"Get a truck, dump a bunch of lumber, and it ends up a house," is an idea he frequently voices. "Same with building a boat. Get a bunch of lumber, and it floats."

* * *

Ernie had the magic hand early when it came to building Snipes, the racing class that first caught his eye while watching a trio of the boats from California dominate the Newport Yacht Club races in Irondequoit Bay in the mid-1930s. His first, *Kiddo*, launched his racing career, his success on Irondequoit Bay prompting him to dip his toe into foreign waters. World War II was on, as was gasoline rationing, and Ernie was still a few months away from deciding to join the navy. He tucked a twenty-gallon drum of gas into *Kiddo*'s cockpit and latched the boat trailer onto the back of the 1940 Plymouth convertible he'd acquired from a guy who'd just signed on with the navy.

"He told me, 'If you make the payments, you can have the car,'" Ernie says.

"He still owed $300 on it, so I considered that a pretty good deal."

He and Ruth piled in with another couple from the Newport Yacht Club, John and Esther O'Brien, and made the three-hundred-mile drive to the North Atlantic Snipe Class Championships on Lake Mohawk, a large artificial body of water in New Jersey.

As Ernie immediately discovered, "It was similar to the bay, which I knew like the back of my hand."

He would be racing against sixteen other boats, and upon his arrival Ernie was informed that there was a home-water favorite.

"They all told me, 'Oh, Beckett's going to win. You came all the way from Rochester to get beat by Beckett?'"

Beckett. Ernie never did learn the man's first name, but he did get a sense of what he was going against.

"He'd have his lackey bring his boat over," Ernie says. "Then he'd drive over in his Cadillac."

Ernie won the first race on Saturday. "I played the wind," he says. "I watched the trees and the clouds."

After winning the day's second race, he was pulling his boat from the water to let it dry out for Sunday's third and final match. A handful of the local wharf rats drifted over, stunned that the mighty Beckett was being shut out on his home waters.

"They said, 'Oh, you can't pull your boat out of the water,'" Ernie says. He ignored them and pulled his boat. The race committee checked out *Kiddo*, this mysterious alien craft, measuring its dimensions, measuring its sails. But everything fell within Snipe parameters.

That last race, "Everybody ganged up on me," Ernie says. "There was hardly any wind, but I thought, if there was going to be any, it looked like it was going to be coming from the stern."

He was right. Laying back, "I caught the wind and sailed around the whole fleet," he says. "It was very exciting for a country bumpkin to go down there and beat all of these doctors and lawyers from New York City."

And he did it with another affront to the homeboys' manhoods. On these two-man boats, Ernie's crewman had been a woman, Esther O'Brien. Her husband and Ruth just came along for the party.

Weeks later, Ernie and *Kiddo* went their separate ways. He sold the boat and joined the navy.

While off in the Pacific, Ernie pondered the intricacies of boatbuilding, which he would put into practice upon his return.

"I had the idea that it was a little too blunt," he says of the Snipe's bow. Starting with the kit skeleton, he slid the second and third frames back an inch apiece, making for a narrower bow. The front piece of the bow was hard oak, to fend off whatever he might encounter floating in the water. But the rest of the boat, "I built it out of very soft wood, western cedar, what they make shingles out of," Ernie says, "because it was light and available."

Diplomatically named *R's*—although Ruth wouldn't be spending a lot of time aboard it—he tweaked his second Snipe until it screamed. This craft was aching to be measured against the best, and in 1946 that meant the nationals, that year being held in the Gulf of Mexico, off Corpus Christi, Texas. Ernie and three other guys in a Buick Roadmaster stacked their two boats—*R's* and *Ghost*—one on top of the other on a trailer for the 1,775-mile ride to Texas.

Early in the drive, the weight of the boats proved to be too much for the trailer, and it began to fold in on itself lengthwise. The guys bought some chains, cinching up the trailer as tight as they could, stopping every now and then to tighten it a little more, until they'd drawn it back into a pretty close approximation of what they'd started with. Ernie drove the final dusk-to-dawn shift. He remembered those long stretches of Texas road interrupted only by bumps where the railroad tracks crossed, until the diamond lights of Gulf Coast oil refineries drew them in to Corpus.

This was a land of extremes. Sun, wind, and waves.

"The local boys had coveralls on and hats with a skirt on the back," Ernie recalls.

"They were covered. I had a good tan, but I got sunburned on top of it."

The nationals were a series of three races with fifty boats nosing toward the starting line. "Very windy," Ernie says. "Extremely windy. The boat in front of me capsized. I'd see it and then it was gone. He was in the trough; I was on the wave. I just missed one guy in the water. Those centerboards are as sharp as a knife, you know.

"I was doing very well. Until the last race. I crossed the starting line one second early." Ernie had to circle back and start again. He needed to place twentieth or better to finish third overall. From dead last, he managed to climb back to thirtieth. Not good enough. *R's* was tenth overall. Nevertheless, "I was very pleased," Ernie says. "It was really rough." Later that summer, after a fourth-place finish in a big set of races at Chautauqua Lake, he sold *R's* on the spot to a guy from New Jersey. No, it wasn't Beckett.

Ernie went to work in the basement on his third Snipe. More tinkering and squabbling. But nothing was going to get in the way of this super Snipe, including asking Ruth for a divorce in the midst of the project.

"I built it extra light, because weight was important," he says. The hull was half-inch cedar once again, rather than oak. The deck quarter-inch plywood. He left the cockpit opening extra large, further reducing weight.

"The weight was below the waterline," Ernie says.

"The weight [or absence of weight] above the waterline is very important. The more water you displace, the more you have to push out of the way with your sail."

He named it *Feather*. As in, light as a feather.

"Boy, that boat was hot," Ernie says. It was also too light for the Snipe class. Ernie had nearly outsmarted himself. Oak floorboards and a bronze centerboard added the necessary thirty pounds, keeping him in fleet championship trophies until he married Evie.

Decades later, as he told the story of his boats, *Feather* was the only one that Ernie knew was still afloat, cruising the lakes in Kansas.

* * *

Ernie had said that *Desire*, his boat for nearly four decades, is not really a racing boat. But he sails it like it is. And *Desire* sails like it wants to be one. "It acts like a Snipe," he says. "It has a big jib and a high boom. That's a Snipe configuration right there.

"And it's unforgiving, like a Snipe. You make a mistake, you're out."

A sailor on another boat had taken a photo of *Desire* winning a race in the fall 2010 series. At age ninety-three, Ernie was not only still sailing, but winning his races. Pointing to the photo, he shows how his all-woman crew is doing the work. One handles the foresail, the triangular sail at the front of the boat fixed to a line that runs from the top of the mast to the bowsprit. Another handles the mainsail, trailing behind the mast. Two other women are in the cockpit with Ernie, dealing with lines, the tiller, and other tasks.

"You watch the curl," Ernie says, pointing to the edge of *Desire*'s white jib. Sloops wear different styles and sizes of foresails, each designed for a different wind: jib, spinnaker, and the extra-large jib, called a genoa. The photo shows that *Desire*'s jib does have a barely perceptible outward curve near the wide top. That means the sail's full, catching all of the wind that it can.

"Like a balloon," Ernie says. "It needs constant attention."

Now he points out the thin black line running the length of the hull, where it meets the water. That's the bootstripe.

"Always, when I'm sailing, I try to keep it on a level line," he says.

"With the spinnaker out, it tends to push the bow down. You want the boat level fore and aft. If the bow is buried, you're not making progress. If the stern is buried, you're not making progress."

Ernie watched a set of levels in the cockpit to ensure the boat is perfectly balanced. Sometimes he'd move the crew members around, using their weight as counterbalances to get it right.

In the photo, the bootstripe is one steady line from bow to stern. *Desire* is perfectly balanced.

What looks like ski poles project from either side of the mast, low enough so that the mainsail boom will sweep over them. These are wind compasses that Ernie added in 1990. Compasses high on the mast—Ernie has those as well—may be misleading. "The wind can vary, ten, seven, eight miles an hour from the top of the mast to the bottom," he says. "There's more wind higher off the water. I go up thirty-six feet." And on the mainsail, unlike what's happening up front with the foresails, it's the wider bottom that's catching the best of the wind, giving the boat the most push. *Desire* is a complex piece of machinery. Ernie read the compasses, the cockpit levels, the telltales dangling from the lines, and the look of the sails to gauge how efficiently *Desire* is moving.

In building Snipes, he tweaked this, adjusted that, found the extra speed. Even though *Desire* was ready to sail from the moment he got his hands on the boat in 1972, Ernie couldn't resist fiddling with it yet again and again. It was an obsession, natural evolution that comes with a craftsman sizing up each boat ahead of him, pondering what he could do to nose his way to the front.

Sharing his secrets while sitting beneath the tulip tree, he'd long ago set aside his carpentry business. Boats had been Ernie's profession for more than a decade. It had been years since he cut a board in someone else's employ.

"I'd decided I'd had enough," he says, as squirrels chatter overhead in the trees, gathering nuts, preparing for winter.

"I went in for myself. Boat repair, because there was plenty of it."

His bad knees weren't allowing him to get down on the deck anymore to do the tough work. But he could sit on a stool and massage the wood fittings, sanding and varnishing until they shined. Or repair a ding in the fiberglass so it matched the original surface. Ernie was a crafty creature emerging from the cavern beneath his home on Madison Terrace with a vial of alchemy, some sandpaper, and an idea of what that boat could become. It is a metaphor for how he'd shaped his life and everything around it for ninety-three years. Perhaps that boat was once a beauty but now needed a little tender loving care. Ernie understood it.

"Think of a blonde," he says, "with a few teeth knocked out."

Hope, the Thames River sailing barge owned by Ernie Coleman's grandparents.

A young Ernie with his mother, May, and stepfather Alfred Kyle.

The East Rochester High glee club. Ernie is the handsome lad in the second row, far right.

The East Rochester High School tennis team. Ernie is in the top row to the left.

The USS *Vincennes* **during maneuvers off Hawaii in June 1942.** *U.S. Naval Archives.*

Ernie's U.S. Navy portrait, 1942.

Ernie sitting in his first snipe, *Kiddo*, in 1947.

Ernie's second wife, Jen.

Ernie with his third wife, Evle, in 1982.

Ernie and his fourth wife, Marilyn, on the slopes of Jackson Hole, Wyoming.

Desire, with the setting sun peeking through its sails.

Desire under full sail on Lake Ontario.

FOURTEEN

The '60s was the instant decade. Instant coffee. Instant vegetables. Reach into the pantry, open a can. American B-52 Stratofortress bombers and Soviet TU-95 Bears pass each other over Arctic airspace with payloads of nuclear weapons, each intent on their Cold War targets. Instant annihilation. A few movies have speculated about where we'd be if those bombers weren't called off in time. *Fail Safe*. And *Dr. Strangelove, or: How I Stopped Worrying and Learned to Love the Bomb.* There may be no more iconic an image for the time than Slim Pickens waving his cowboy hat as he sits astride a huge bomb, riding it to nuclear Armageddon.

For Ernie, it was a decade of instant family. Upon marrying Evie in 1961, he and Pat were suddenly living in a very full house of Ross kids.

He wasn't immediately embraced as a family member, Ernie admits. Evie's kids had lost their father a few years earlier, and now here was another man moving in and bringing a five-year-old with him as well.

"It wasn't easy," Ernie says. "The older boy was thirteen at the time; he was the father of the outfit." Charlie didn't outwardly reject the new arrangement, Ernie says, but "He was a hard kid to talk to anyway."

Nevertheless, "I just loved it," Ernie says. "Evie and I used to have a lot of battles over my discipline. She'd say, 'The kids will never love you.' I told her I didn't care if they loved me as long as they respected me.

"She had an expression, 'If you do that, I'm gonna kill you.' She never killed anybody. I told the kids, 'You lie to me, you're going to pay for it.'

Well, one of the kids lied to me. I pulled his pants down, put him over my knee. I didn't hurt him, but he felt it."

Taking his new role as dad to Evie's kids seriously, Ernie sold the last of his Snipes, *Feather*, in 1961, soon to be replaced by a junk 1952 Plymouth. Junk to most people—a seemingly useless carcass but a learning experience for Ernie's two newly acquired teenage sons to pick over. Put some focus in their lives.

"There were a few hundred acres of field out back, toward the railroad tracks," says Charlie, Evie's recalcitrant older son. "It was for us to learn how to take apart and put back together, learn about engines, and to drive around in the field. He always thought it's useful to have a skill like that."

Ernie's ideas of raising a family fell in line with his own personal philosophy: keep busy. He and Evie kept his Summerville connection alive with the first of the two summer cottages they would purchase on Madison Terrace and rent out, even as Ernie renovated it into a year-round home. And they quickly plotted out an unusual arrangement with their renters. As soon as the kids were out of school, the families swapped homes. Evie, Ernie, and the kids spent the summer living on Madison Terrace, with Ernie continuing his renovations. This worked great for a few summers until the Vietnam War interceded, and the renters, conscientious objectors to the war—and one of whom was of draft age—left for Canada.

Ernie wasn't as fortunate with the next renter, "a deadbeat," Ernie says. "He didn't pay his rent and left a broken-down car in the front yard. I had to hire a lawyer to get him out of there. He was a headache."

Feather may have been gone, but Ernie slowly drifted back to the prevailing winds of Lake Ontario. He was determined to take a couple of the kids with him. Evie, too, if the winds were really working in his favor. In much the same way that he had dragged home the near-comatose Plymouth, Ernie returned one day from a remodeling job, having partially settled the bill by taking off the customer's hands a homemade plywood sailboat, stored in the garage and painted what Jan remembers as "state park green."

"That's what he started to teach us to sail on," she says. "We used to carry the mast home, and he locked up the boat with a chain on the beach. Then someone stole it."

Perhaps that setback was for the best.

"It leaked a little bit," she says.

Soon enough, while on another job, Ernie spotted yet another sailboat languishing in a garage. This was a Sunfish, a thirteen footer much smaller and easier to move around than a Snipe.

"Never been used," Ernie says. "I offered to buy it from him, he deducted it from the bill, and I brought it home. I had the kids in mind."

Truth be told, Ernie had himself in mind as well. He piled on board with his two youngest girls, Jan and Pat. That's how they began sailing the regattas. Ernie and a boatload of girls. The one-person Sunfish was a perfect fit.

"You've got to be pretty athletic to sail it," Ernie says. "They flip over pretty good."

His way of showing the girls how to deal with a dunking was by taking them out into the lake and deliberately dumping the boat. That's how you learn how to get back on board.

Evie never would have stood for that.

"She didn't like it when the boat heeled over," Ernie says. "We'd get over five degrees, she'd say, 'Straighten it up.'"

Although the Sunfish was light enough to run up on the beach at the end of Madison Terrace, Ernie didn't feel comfortable leaving it there. He bought a trailer, rented a garage at a nearby apartment complex, and was soon dragging the Sunfish to yacht clubs up and down the lakeshore for races.

The sailors in the family turned out to be Jan, Pat, and Charlie. And later, after he married Marilyn, her daughter, Julie.

"Julie took to it," Jan says. "She was a natural at it. I'm good at it because I love it. She's good at it because she's a natural. Tricia and Julie, they can put the math-science thing behind it. I just wing it."

When Jan and Pat graduated together from Irondequoit High School in 1974, Pat went off to a nearby college, studying two years to become a nurse.

"This is a kid who couldn't stand the sight of blood," Ernie says. "Where is she now? The operating room." In Phoenix. Pat had drifted to the Southwest, far from her father's sailing world on Lake Ontario.

Jan remained in Rochester. Ernie sold the Sunfish and added *Desire* to the family, and she became an enthusiastic and increasingly important member of *Desire*'s crew.

"I wouldn't be sailing without her," Ernie says. "She fits the boat out in the spring, organizes the crew."

Jan's a familiar figure around the Genesee Yacht Club, a by-product of her crewing on *Desire* and her gregarious personality when she's hanging out at the modest clubhouse. It was Ernie's environment, and it became Jan's as well.

Charlie is different. He finds comfort in the more moneyed Rochester Yacht Club, working his way up to a two-year term as club commodore. Even during non-sailing season, the evenings in the RYC clubhouse can roar with conversation, as landlocked sailors sit at the bar, ordering food and drinks, waiting for spring to arrive and the day they can get their boats back in the water.

Charlie got into sailing late, and not because of any direct influence from his stepdad.

"I didn't know anything about his sailing as a kid," Charlie says. Already a teenager when Ernie arrived, he was going his own way, eventually finding the path to a thirty-eight-year career at Eastman Kodak.

But by the mid-'70s, he was spending time on friends' boats. Sailing was a social thing. Steer in a circle a few miles out from port, "have a cocktail, that sort of thing," Charlie says. Before long, he was racing on a friend's veteran Soling, a twenty-seven-foot racing boat, a design known for competing in the Olympics. This one had lost its Olympian edge.

"I kept asking, 'Why isn't this boat competitive?'" Charlie says. "And my friend says, 'It's old.'"

So they split the cost of a newer Soling before Charlie graduated to a J/24, while also crewing twenty-four years on one of the grandest yachts at the club, the forty-seven-foot, black-hulled, Bruce Farr–designed racing boat *Rampage*. A creature of technology, the antithesis of Ernie's instincts.

Charlie mulls over a proper description of Ernie's old-school style.

"I don't know if instinct is the right word," he says. "His senses are very acute to wind speed and wind changes. He can feel it on his face, on the back of his neck, on his nose."

"He's so in tune with it, sometimes he gets a little intense," Jan says. Particularly at the start of a race, what Ernie calls "'threading the needle,' when he gets to the starting line and ducks between these big boats, and you think there's no way he's gonna make it. And he does."

Almost always. Charlie remembers Ernie proudly showing off his new *Desire* by taking a few family members out to get a close look at Turtle Rock, a large, flat obstruction two hundred feet or so off the shoreline. It generally lies just below the surface of the lake but peeks out when the water level is low, usually in the fall. In one of Ernie's rare moments of sailing misjudgment, he ran *Desire* right over the top of Turtle Rock and got stuck.

"The coast guard had to send a boat over to get us off," Charlie says. "They had to fire a line over to us, because they couldn't get any closer. I always like to remind him of that."

FIFTEEN

Most mornings of their married life—thirty-five years—the first thing Ernie saw upon walking into the kitchen each morning before going off to work was Evie's cigarette smoldering in an ashtray.

Nothing unusual there. In 1965, 42 percent of Americans smoked cigarettes. Ernie himself had picked up the habit during his second stint in the navy. But Evie? "She smoked all her life," Ernie says. "She'd get up, the first thing she would do was light a cigarette."

Disciplining the kids was sometimes a matter of "Do as I say, not as I do."

Ernie was usually out of the house and on his way to a job site by the time the school bus pulled up in front of the house. But one morning he was running late, unbeknownst to the two boys who had stepped behind the house to smoke cigarettes. They routinely opened Evie's cigarette cartons from the bottom and slipped out a few, figuring she wouldn't notice they were gone. The boys immediately snuffed out their smokes when they heard Ernie coming out of the house that morning, but he knew the game. They were busted.

"They asked Evie, 'How come he knows so much about this stuff?'" Ernie says. "She said, 'He was your age once.'"

It wasn't as if Evie and Ernie didn't understand the dangers of smoking. They knew, instructing their kids to stay away from cigarettes, even as Ernie and Evie took their chances, as do many folks. I told Ernie how, as a young teenager, I used to go down to the basement where my dad spent a lot of time because my parents didn't speak to each other for a few years. I'd smell smoke and spot him hovering over his tools, discreetly smashing out a butt in a coffee can. Neither one of us commented on it. I'd just pick up a screwdriver or whatever it was I was after and go back upstairs, thinking: "I'm the teenage kid, I'm supposed to be the one who's been caught smoking."

Ernie thought that story was funny, especially after I told him that I'd made my dad an ashtray in shop class one year.

* * *

Evie may have been no fan of sailboats heeling in the wind, but the social whirl of a yacht club with a solid foundation suited her just fine. A year after buying *Desire*, they joined the Genesee Yacht Club. This was a budget-friendly decision. The Rochester Yacht Club's dues were out of the reach of their modest, middle-class income. And at GYC, Evie found a comrade who, like her, didn't like rocking the boat. An outgoing sort, Evie had befriended Inez Law. Inez's husband Paul had a big thirty-four-foot racing sailboat, but Inez would have no part of it.

"She'd sleep on the boat but couldn't handle the motion when it was moving," Ernie says of Inez. "She would drive from one port to the next when we were sailing."

Bowling was the sport favored by the two women. Evie even watched it on television. Inez and Evie dragged their husbands into a mixed Friday-night league, where Evie once rolled a 276 game.

They were out bowling one night when Ernie got a phone call at the lanes. Ruth was dead. She'd remarried, but her husband had died some six months earlier. Ruth had been living alone and was found at the bottom of a staircase, apparently having tripped and fallen to her death.

"Her sister thought it was foul play," Ernie says quietly.

He was not a conspiracy theorist. As Ernie retells Evie's story in the fall of 2010, he adds that he'd been at Inez Law's funeral five days earlier. She died of a brain tumor.

* * *

The older you get, the deeper grows the warehouse of souls. It took a decade for the final drama of Evie's life to unfold, but a lifetime of smoking caught up with her. Evie's doctor tried to head it off, ordering her to quit in 1985 as the pressure in Evie's left eye grew increasingly elevated. Ernie stopped smoking as well, "because she had to," he says. "I really missed it. It was difficult. I used to bum a cigarette every so often for a while."

Four operations couldn't save Evie's eye. The retina detached and she went blind in that eye.

"Nobody knew it," Ernie says. "She did a good job of hiding it."

They were considering getting Evie a glass eye when, after ignoring some nagging concerns, she finally went for a mammogram. Maybe the drama of her eye troubles had been enough to keep her from pursuing more bad news. But Evie, Ernie says, "kept putting it off, because she was afraid she had cancer."

Unfortunately, Evie's self-diagnosis was correct. Ernie took her for her mammogram at 9 in the morning. They didn't get home until 10 p.m. that night. Her mammogram showed a dark spot on her lung. When they returned to Rochester General Hospital, doctors went for a biopsy through her back, inadvertently collapsing a lung in the process, and Evie spent a few days in the hospital recovering. The tests came back in two weeks, confirming the tumor was malignant.

Still, her doctors predicted she had a 95 percent chance of survival.

Radiation treatment is scary business now, and it was doubly so in 1995.

"Radiation kills the cancer cells," Ernie says. "It also kills the cells around it. The scar tissue collected around her lungs." That meant her lungs' ability to process oxygen was compromised.

With each disappointing visit to her doctors, it was becoming clearer that Evie would be among that 5 percent of non-survivors. While she was being treated, Ernie would stand outside the hospital, watching others.

"People were under the canopy, smoking like a chimney," he says. "And they were all working there! I still see them up there smoking, when I have the occasion to go there. Smoking in their white outfits."

Evie was on oxygen now, "cords all over the house," Ernie says.

She was suffocating.

"She was never in any pain—pain from the cancer. She had anxiety attacks because she couldn't catch her breath."

Ernie set her up in a hospital bed in the first-floor family room that he'd added on to their home, the renovation that had been a part of the plan for spending their lives together.

"I rigged up a bell system so she could reach up and press a button when I wasn't in the room," he says.

"I had another bell downstairs in the shop."

Hospice workers came for a couple of hours every day. Judy spent every Tuesday with her mother.

"I needed it. It was rough," Ernie says. "I needed that four hours to myself."

Evie fell into a coma her final two days.

"I thought: she's gonna die of starvation," Ernie says.

He went for a walk while Evie's oldest son Charlie, his wife Betsey, and their youngest daughter Kate stayed at the house. Ernie wandered down the street, lost in the inevitable.

"They hollered, 'Come on back!'" Ernie recalls. He was too late.

"She died with her eyes wide open. That really bothered me. We had to close them."

SIXTEEN

The life had gone out of the house on Madison Terrace with Evie's death. Ernie's response was to move all of the furniture aside in the family room, where she had spent her final days. He threw blankets over everything and set up a net against one of the walls.

"I covered the west window with heavy cardboard, and I would practice golf by the hour," he says. Whiling away the time, hitting one golf ball, then the next, then the next. He did this for months. His daughter Judy came to visit.

"This looks like a bachelor's pad," she said.

"Well, I guess it is," Ernie said.

By February 1996, the bleakness of the Rochester winter was squeezing Ernie like a fist. Bored, he closed up the house and drove to Florida, visiting friends and his brother Frank. He played a little golf, although the indoor sessions had hardly raised him to touring-pro level.

"If I break 100, I'm happy," he says.

When he returned to Rochester, "I buried myself in work. Seven days a week. Painting bottoms, waxing hulls, doing varnish work."

But by June, he knew: "I can't stand this living alone. I'm not a guy for living alone. I like company."

He began reading the classified section of the newspaper. The personals.

"You just look down the list, 'Women Wanting Men,'" he says. Just like buying a car or some tools.

"I found one that said, 'I like skiing and sailing,' something like that. So I answered the ad.

"Marilyn called, said she'd like to meet me, and we set a date to have coffee. Half an hour later, she called back and said, 'Why don't you just come to the house?'"

Marilyn's thirty-year marriage had fallen apart a couple of years earlier. After a year of feeling sorry for herself, she'd started moving on with her life, trying singles groups. Parents without Partners, that didn't work. So she tried the personals. This direct-marketing approach worked fine. Marilyn received twenty-eight responses.

But the quality of the pool left something to be desired. The first twenty-seven didn't measure up in one respect or another. Everyone was carrying some kind of baggage. Except, perhaps, this last one, Ernie. He had potential. Her ad read that she was looking for a first mate. He had a boat and an interest in learning how to ski.

Ernie showed up at her house with a bottle of red wine and a bottle of white. Marilyn did a quick evaluation when she answered the door. He was kind of sailor-like in appearance with his white beard and mustache, wearing what she calls "a funny Greek sailing cap." And he didn't appear to fall within the age range that her ad had called for, fifty-five to sixty-five. He was to the December side of that. Nevertheless, she let him in. Didn't want to hurt his feelings.

"She talked me into cooking steaks," Ernie says. "By midnight, the wine was gone. I was a mellow fellow. I took my time driving home.

"She was so friendly and so outgoing. I was impressed."

They quickly became friends. And friends were all they could be, Marilyn warned Ernie. There seemed to be too much of an age difference. She still wasn't sure how much. Is it rude to ask?

The friendship was in place, but Ernie hadn't signed any contracts defining their relationship. After a few evenings at his house serving his two dinner specialties—chili and stew—he made his move.

"I asked her, 'How would you like to go sailing on *Desire*?'"

From there, "Every date we had was to go sailing." Ernie had the wind at his back now, and he needed it. At fifty-five, she was much younger than Ernie.

"I didn't tell her I was almost eighty," he says. "She didn't ask me."

Marilyn strolls into the kitchen where Ernie's sitting at the table discussing their courtship.

"All the guys I was dating ended up being such losers," she says. "So I always ended up coming here. That must have told me something."

The sailing season was coming to a close that first year of their relationship, and Ernie's kids were planning on celebrating his birthday on November 20. Ernie was plotting otherwise. Ernie knew Marilyn, a travel agent, was putting together a singles cruise for a local ski club that would have her gone during his birthday.

"Think there's room for me?" he asked.

"Dead silence."

She didn't have the heart to tell Ernie that he was too old for a singles cruise. Even if the singles were in their fifties and a decade beyond that. She relented.

"I called up the kids, postponed the party for a week," Ernie says. "That's when she found out how old I was, when I told her my kids were planning an eightieth birthday party for me."

Marilyn's reaction?

Ernie smiles. "'Gulp. . . .'"

This would be yet another challenge. Like building his first boat. Or he and *Kiddo* trekking three hundred miles to take on the mighty Beckett on his home waters of Lake Mohawk. And on the cruise, Ernie met the challenge once again. He had to prove to Marilyn tnat he wasn't some old man watching life from a distance.

"We were on the ship with all of these young guys, and by 9 o'clock they're in the sack asleep or whatever," Ernie says. "I'm up there dancing. I guess she was impressed with that. She told me later, 'Somehow, you managed to turn that around.' Anyway, it was a happy ending."

Ernie wasn't through. He announced to Marilyn that he was ready to take up skiing as well. After six lessons, he was hitting the intermediate trails.

"I'd always wanted to ski, but I couldn't afford it," he says. "But the kids were gone, and I was alone now. And I really loved it. She dragged me out to Jackson Hole, Wyoming. I enjoyed it. I didn't do anything crazy."

The relationship was progressing nicely. Ernie was proving to be a durable travel partner for his travel-agent girlfriend Marilyn.

One weekend, rather than bothering to go home, Marilyn simply stayed at Ernie's place.

"I thought, 'Oh, wow, this is interesting,'" Ernie says. By late spring '97, "She started spending every weekend here. Things were getting better and better."

Now it was Ernie's turn to set some parameters.

"I told her I'm not looking for marriage," he says. "I'm a jinx. I married three women. I don't want to put that curse on a fourth."

Nevertheless, he began converting an upstairs bedroom into an office for Marilyn.

"Her ivory tower," he calls it, where she could do telemarketing work. Before long, "She moved in with me," he says. "The kids all approved. I also told them I was spending their inheritance. They said they didn't need it anyway."

The old folks were shacking up.

Getting married "was kind of her idea, I think," Ernie says. "She needed some kind of security. I'm an old geezer. What if I pass away? So one day I said to her, 'Let's get hitched.' Then I thought, 'That's a hell of a thing to say.'"

He tried it again, with a more romantic approach: "'Sweetie, would you marry me?'

"The next day, I went out and bought her an engagement ring. She picked it out."

After a five-year courtship, they were married on October 20, 2001. In what was Ernie's well-practiced routine, they went to a justice of the peace.

"Love, honor, and obey," Ernie says. "Well, strike that 'obey.'"

The next month, they and 177 guests celebrated a combination wedding reception and Ernie's eighty-fifth birthday party at the Rochester Yacht Club.

"Charlie had an SUV there to bring the stuff back to the house, and it was loaded," Ernie says. "It took us two days to go through it. Needless to say, there was a lot of booze. We didn't need to buy anything for six months."

SEVENTEEN

"**F**lyboys," he calls them.

Ernie remembers standing outside the Maui base one beautiful clear morning watching a group of seven of them—"they were young kids"—hot-rodding over the landscape in their Grumman F6F Wildcat fighters, perhaps twenty miles distant, soaring straight toward the Haleakala volcano.

"All seven of them didn't pull up quickly enough," Ernie says. "You could see them trying to pull up, but thcy were following the leader."

His hand traces the flight path of each fighter plane, soaring and abruptly ending in the side of Haleakala.

"It was like watching a movie," he says. "Nobody made it."

A call came in to the carpenter's shop a few hours later. The bodies had been recovered; seven rough boxes were needed. The carpenters called a guy out of the brig, a common practice when they found themselves shorthanded. The only stipulation was that the carpenters had to promise to take the prisoner back. Ernie had him lie down on a four-by-eight sheet of plywood so he could trace out a basic coffin shape. When the guy figured out what was going on, he leaped to his feet in fear. He wasn't going to be used as a template for death.

This memory probably goes back to 1944. Thirty-one years later, in 1975, Ernie returned to Hawaii. He was fifty-five years old. Who knew how much time he had remaining on the old clock? He chose Hawaii, he says, "to see the place where I spent twenty-two months. Show Evie all about it."

And perhaps to remind himself that he had once been a part of something that was really big. He'd been a player in important history. One of those Greatest Generation guys, even if he was reluctant to talk about it.

They flew to Honolulu in a 747, "the first time I ever saw one," Ernie says. "Boy, the engines on that thing. They're monster things." He heard tell of a mystical second level in that aircraft, up a spiral staircase at the front of the plane where other passengers enjoyed their cocktails as they soared thirty thousand feet over the Pacific Ocean. Ernie was just a guy who fixed boats so, "needless to say, we didn't go first class."

But they were first-class tourists. They peered into Mauna Loa, the world's largest volcano, on the Big Island of Hawaii.

"It was bubbling at the time we were there," Ernie says.

The chances of Ernie and Evie getting roasted were unlikely, as Mauna Loa's eruptions are quite mild. Yet, "the smell of sulfur was horrible," he says. "They didn't let you stay long. You would be asphyxiated."

The island of Maui, where he'd spent his time, was of more interest. Ernie's recollection of the old whaling port of Lahaina from his navy days was that there weren't any whales to be seen. Many years later, he'd heard on a Jacques Cousteau television documentary that fish won't come within one hundred miles of water where dynamite has exploded.

"Since it's only ninety miles from Pearl Harbor," Ernie says of Lahaina, "there was a lot of dynamite in the water."

But now, Ernie saw that whale watching was a big industry in Lahaina. All had been forgiven between nature and the planet's angriest inhabitants, at least in that pleasant corner of the world.

"Apparently the ocean cleared it up," he says.

The memories were thicker still around Haleakala volcano, deep in dormant slumber, its old lava flows wrapped around it like a blanket. During the war, this is where sailors were sent for R & R. And target practice.

"They wanted us to shoot the goats," Ernie says. "They were propagating so badly, they were coming out of the crater and eating the pineapples."

Ernie recalled for Evie how he and four of his navy pals packed three days' worth of food and hiked up to the ranger cabins. From the ten-thousand-foot summit, they could look down and watch the flyboys scooting low along the valley at the foot of the mountain, the Wildcats literally at their feet.

"They were a pretty good match for the Zero," Ernie says of the legendary Japanese fighter plane, "because they were maneuverable. The F4s, too, but they added heavier armaments to the F6." As usual, Ernie knows his specs.

The goat squad was warned it would be cold up on Haleakala, and that proved to be true. Ernie remembers waking up the first morning and blowing on his eyeglasses, hoping to raise a little condensation so that he could clean them off. But even though he saw a thin layer of ice on top of the rainwater collection barrels at the ranger cabins, "you couldn't even see your breath, that's how dry it was up there."

At these elevations, and only on the Hawaiian volcanic summits of Haleakala and Mauna Kea, grow the beautiful silver-green colored silversword. Ernie noticed that the narrow leaves on one silversword, which blooms in an exotic ball, were moving in an odd way. Poking about, he discovered that air was blowing out of mysterious holes in the long-hardened lava. Tubes big enough to admit a man.

For a kid who'd tested himself time and again against what Lake Ontario had to offer, this was too exotic a sight to resist.

"I said, 'You want to go down there?' I want to see what this is all about.'" With flashlight beams pointing the way, Ernie led two of the guys into the tube, which soon expanded into a space the size of the kitchen where he sat recalling this adventure. "I told them, 'No hollering, or it might fall on us.'"

These channels are the result of the lava flow itself. When an eruption ends, the lava drains back down the slope and into the volcano, leaving the tubes clear. And these tubes can be extraordinarily long. One of Mauna Loa's is thirty-one miles. They kept pushing farther into the volcanic passage, perhaps 150 yards. Even there, Ernie still could feel a breeze blowing from the tube, but it had grown too narrow and they were forced to turn back.

There was a massacre to tend to, anyway. The navy men took their carbines into a crater and one of them spotted a goat peering over a steep cliff. Everyone opened fire.

"I'll bet that head had fifteen shots in it," Ernie says. "You'd think it was a battle up there."

They were just young guys, cutting loose after experiencing war, the worst that humanity can offer.

But some of Ernie's images of R & R on Maui were unsettling. He has a memory of the Fourth Marines returning from Iwo Jima, and how a handful of them went on rampage, killing nine Japanese American civilians "because they were trained to kill Japanese," Ernie says. "They had to be quarantined, to straighten those guys out. It was horrible."

* * *

During the first half of his life, adventure abroad came infrequently for Ernie, considering his heavy schedule of renovating houses and boats, sailing, scaring the neighborhood kids on Halloween wearing his gorilla suit, and, after marrying Evie, raising a big family. His travels had generally been modest or government subsidized. Big vacations were an irresponsible use of time and money for a Great Depression kid. But as he began to reach out and explore the world, his excursions were never far from water.

He took his first cruise in 1969 aboard *Rotterdam*.

"When the ship was the old rules," Ernie says. "If you didn't have a tux on for the captain's dinner, you don't go."

The seven-day voyage left New York City and motored through Cape Hatteras down to Freeport, Nassau, and Bermuda.

Rotterdam was a Dutch ship, and "all they had on board was Heineken," Ernie says. He's not complaining. "Seven-point-five cents a glass. I don't know where they got the half cent. All you had to do was tell them your cabin number."

This lifestyle went down easy with Ernie. Friends like Bill and Barb, an English couple who house-sat for them, helped ease his mind about being away from home. Someone had to feed the alarm. "Bill went out one night and the dog wouldn't let him back in," Ernie says.

Bill and Barb eventually moved back to England, and years later Ernie the late-blooming globetrotter was now regretting not taking them up on an offer to visit.

"I never got around to it, seeing my heritage," he says. "I'll probably never see England."

Instead, Ernie and Evie tried cruises to Puerto Rico and another on *Pacific Princess* through the Panama Canal. That canal still rankled the casual historian in Ernie.

"We built the thing, then we gave it away," he says severely.

Pacific Princess was the original star of the mid-'70s through '80s TV series *The Love Boat*, but such idyllic creations can only insulate so much from the outside world. It was while sailing on *Pacific Princess* that Ernie and Evie heard the news that the United States had invaded Iraq. Desert Storm was on.

It was only after he turned eighty in 1996 that Ernie emerged as a true world sightseer. Marilyn organized tours to all sorts of exotic destinations. Even before they married, Ernie had been tagging along: The Dominican Republic, where Marilyn hired a young pilot with braces on his teeth to fly a helicopter up and down the beach while she scouted potential resorts for her clients. Antigua, where Ernie got involved in the resort's daily Hobie Cat competitions on the beach, winning every race with the small catamarans. His prize: a bottle of rum. There was two weeks in Italy, with which he fell in love. Then Germany, Austria, and Switzerland. They visited Tahiti and the Polynesian islands—"very hot, not much to see," Ernie says dismissively. And cruises to St. Maarten, Venice, Croatia, Greece, Majorca, Tunisia, Barcelona, France, and Alaska, which also required hops on a helicopter and seaplane. There was Sedona, Arizona, beautiful in its rocky landscape and artist studios, and the ski trip to Jackson Hole.

But now there would be no more winter sports. After three years on the slopes, Ernie had to hang up the skis. Doctor's orders; too rough on his well-worn knees and heart.

"Giving that up was the hardest thing I had to do," he says.

And it was in Switzerland, while riding a train to the Matterhorn, at about nine thousand feet altitude, that Ernie realized he couldn't breathe, forcing a retreat by train down to six thousand feet. With worldliness comes age.

And with further passage of time, Ernie needed a wheelchair to get through airports in a timely fashion.

But alternatives were at hand, trips at more reasonable altitudes that didn't include too much walking. In 2008, Marilyn discovered *Royal Clipper*, the largest sailing vessel in the world, manned by a crew drawn from countries throughout Europe. It's Lord Nelson meets *The Love Boat*, with three swimming pools. Morning gymnastics with Maria. Captain Sergey's Story Time on the bridge. Snorkel safaris, mast climbing, and deck golf with the Sports Team. Land excursions to Mount Etna ("please wear comfortable, closed shoes"). Dolphin watching with marine biologist Clara. Compulsory lifeboat drill. And Cocktail Melodies with Tanya and Kunya followed by Pirate Night in the Tropical Bar ("come dressed as a pirate ready for dinner"). All guided by state-of-the-art navigation equipment.

"And the food?" Ernie rolls his eyes and rubs his belly. After growing up during the Great Depression, extravagant food looks like a miracle.

"If you go away hungry from that place, it's your own fault," he says. "I took fish every time. Salmon, mahi-mahi, sea bass, flounder, grouper. The desserts, I gained three pounds in two days. I had to stop eating dessert; my belt was getting too tight. The last night, they came out with baked Alaska, parading around with it, candles and so forth."

This was a vacation that appealed to the old sailor if not his cardiologist, who was concerned with his patient's insistence that he could handle scampering around on the ruins of ancient civilizations.

"Needless to say, I got my sea legs back after two days," Ernie proudly says. "I'm walking a straight line, and they're staggering."

Ernie and Marilyn returned to the ship in 2009 and 2010. Their third voyage on *Royal Clipper* was seven days of noodling around the Mediterranean.

"This is Italy, theoretically," Ernie says, sketching a map on a legal pad. He'll never make it as a cartographer, but it's all there: Naples, the Tyrrhenian Sea, the Aeolian Islands with their two active volcanoes. The Strait of Messina, the 1.8-mile waterway between Sardinia and the boot of Italy.

"They're talking about building a bridge over that," he says.

Since his heart condition emerged, "I can't travel very far," Ernie says. "If I walked from here to the end of the street"—about 150 yards—"I'd have to stop."

But from the boat he could gaze at sights such as Italy's Amalfi Coast, once a vacation spot for royalty.

"Of course, now it's a tourist trap," Ernie says. "How those Italians build on the side of those mountains, I don't know. It's twelve hundred steps to their houses; can you imagine carrying groceries up there?"

Ernie appreciated such industrious aspects of humanity. He generally didn't sound like a Fascist, but he'd say admiringly, "Mussolini did an awful lot with that country to modernize it."

To the old sailor, *Royal Clipper* was a modern marvel. He toured the engine room below, a miracle of cramped engineering with three diesel engines, in case the wind has another assignment at any given moment.

But overhead is the truly breathtaking sight: five masts filled with forty-two stunning white sails, including nine elegant staysails.

"They stick out like a jib off the main mast," Ernie explains. "Of course, when we were going downwind, the staysails aren't doing anything. They're just decoration. People took pictures anyway. It had the effect."

He watched the more daring sailor-tourists climb a mast into the crow's nest.

"They put a belt on you, so if you misstep, you don't fall in the drink," Ernie says.

He watched a young female member of the crew scamper up the mast to the highest yardarm then walk out onto it, taking photographs.

"I thought, 'This girl is crazy.'"

As Ernie has said, no two sails are alike. Nor are they equal. On that third voyage, sails as decoration and masts as a gymnastics venue weren't enough for Ernie.

"I wasn't too thrilled with this one," Ernie says. Not enough wind for good sailing meant the diesels were running too much. "There were areas we couldn't sail because we headed into the wind. We had to motor," he complains. A steady, if not-too-thrilling, 11½ to 12 knots.

Much like a golfer for whom one or two nice shots over eighteen holes is encouragement enough to return to the course, Ernie twice returned to *Royal Clipper* in search of the miracle of his first voyage, a journey that departed from Barbados with stops at Granada, Saint Lucia, and Saint Vincent. Searching for the moment that must have felt like the height of his sport, when, for a half hour, *Royal Clipper*'s captain allowed Ernie to take the helm of a ship that was one and a third football fields longer than the old sailor's twenty-six-foot *Desire*.

Even more, Ernie was searching for a return to the first moments of that first cruise. *Royal Clipper* left port at about 5 p.m. The ship was about eight to ten miles out, cruising at 5 or 6 knots. The sun was sliding away over the horizon, and Ernie took note of the music playing on speakers throughout the ship: Vangelis's overture for the film *1492*. *Royal Clipper* caught the wave swells in perfect time to the swelling of the music.

"The sails started coming down. Oh, it was breathtaking," Ernie says. "You can't explain it, you have to experience it. I think about it; it brings tears to my eyes. It was one of the most memorable moments in my life."

EIGHTEEN

Ernie's lesson for the new millennium: your odometer doesn't hit the eight-decade mark without things going wrong.

Ernie was discovering that in a big way now. Even parties were getting dangerous. Games where a guy sits with a balloon on his lap and, in what must surely be a challenge to personal dignity, his partner bounces on him and attempts to break it. Ernie and Marilyn were pulled into the competition at an Antiguan resort during a 2004 travel-agent junket.

"She jumped on my lap and pushed me right over," Ernie says.

He knew immediately something in his back had gone awry.

"I wasn't going to have an X-ray there," he says, wary of exposing himself to the care of anyone but American doctors. "I laid down for an hour and I couldn't get back up."

That would remain the pattern when Ernie returned to Rochester. He was forced to sleep sitting upright on the couch, his feet stretched out on an ottoman. He tried physical therapy and a chiropractor.

"Nothing worked," Ernie says. "We were considering acupuncture. We had a name of a guy and everything."

Although, oddly, he could still play golf.

This was a new way of life, and Ernie grudgingly accepted it.

"I had never had a broken bone or anything," he says. "I never even took an aspirin, even if I had a headache. I was not a pill popper."

He shrugs. "Now I'm taking them all the time. It keeps me going. I'm not about to stop now."

* * *

Ernie's brother, four years older, was still puttering along in a lucid manner in his Florida apartment. He hated the upstate New York weather and moved to Florida for the year-round golf.

But now, "I'm no longer physically able to swing a golf club," Frank complains.

He is ninety-eight when I give him a call, curious as to how the Coleman genes are holding up. Frank's mind seems reasonably solid, although he can't remember how many times he's been married.

"Let's see, twice maybe? Three times? I don't really know. I've lost track. . . ."

One of his four sons, Larry, gets on the phone to provide the correct answer: once. After Frank's wife Margaret died in 1996, he had a girlfriend for about ten years, until she passed away unexpectedly. Well, maybe the better word there is passed away *suddenly*. We all expect to die one day. Now Larry had moved in to lend a hand. These Coleman boys seemed to have figured out the secret of longevity. Whatever it is.

"I've been asked that question many times, because I'm getting pretty close to the one-hundred mark," Frank says.

It wasn't because he and his brother shared a common environment. They were separated during the Depression, Ernie raised by his mother and stepfather and Frank by his grandparents.

"He went his way and I went mine," Frank says.

Eating right?

"I don't think either one of us has been particularly careful about diet," Frank says.

Perhaps long life is in the genes? "Not really," Ernie says. "My grandmother was ninety-nine, and she was still keeping house. That's about it."

When he hit his eighties, Ernie had a few lesions dug from his cheek, cysts pried from his shoulder, a chunk of his colon removed, two knee replacements, repairs on a broken femur and broken ribs. He added a set of hearing aids. He was even hit by a train while vacationing in the Caribbean. True, it was one of those little tourist trains, more like a string of golf carts, but that'll still leave a bruise. Ernie handled it all with such élan that a Rochester rehabilitation center used his big, smiling face in a newspaper ad touting its services.

Ernie discusses these violations of his body in the same nuts-and-bolts manner as he does the repairs on a sailboat. The colon operation, for example: he spotted blood in a couple of bowel movements and subsequent tests detected cancer. Ernie explains how fourteen inches of his colon were sawed away, then the two ends reattached as easily as you'd fit together a pair of PVC pipes.

He has home remedies as well. It took four operations over a seven-month period to remove a cyst from his shoulder, and the usual gauze and tape couldn't stem the seepage from the wound. Ernie found that binding the area with sanitary napkins worked wonderfully.

Ernie sometimes set himself up for these troubles. In the spring of 2003, the Rochester Yacht Club was burying a sixty-five-foot-long plastic pipe across the harbor entrance, a rig designed to release a stream of bubbles to knock down silt before it flowed into the dock area. A crew of about thirty guys, including a diver, had assembled for the job. Intent on taking photos, Ernie climbed a small hill overlooking the project. It was a cold day, and the ground had frozen into mud ruts. Ernie stumbled and fell. Someone called 911, and an ambulance carried him off to Rochester General Hospital. Diagnosis: broken femur, five inches below his hip.

"They gave me pain pills, but I had a very rough night," he says.

The doctors put him in traction. For the surgery he requested local anesthesia because, "I don't like to get knocked out.

"It didn't hurt," he says. "You feel the action." The splintered bone was wrapped in stainless-steel wire to hold it together. Ernie'd seen guys in the service who were wounded in action bolted together in this manner.

Local anesthesia meant the surgeons had to follow not only their procedures, but Ernie's years of carpentry experience as well.

"Make sure you get those legs the same length," he instructed.

"The guy says, 'You think I'm some kid? I don't know how to use a ruler?'"

Hammers were brought out to put the screws in place that would hold the metal rod in his leg to the broken bone. "You use a screwdriver for a screw," Ernie admonished the surgeon as he tapped away with a mallet. He did, once the screws were in place. The pins, Ernie learned, have threads only near the head.

More work would be needed on Ernie's undercarriage. The years had caught up to the cartilage in his knees.

"My legs were so bowed, they looked like parentheses," he says. "I figured, what the heck, why don't I go for broke?"

However, Ernie did express concern that knee replacements presented an engineering problem with his newly repaired femur.

"Stainless-steel rod meets a titanium knee," he says. "That's two incompatible metals." Ernie could solve this problem. "Put a piece of zinc between the two and you won't have that galvanic reaction," he helpfully suggested.

Fortunately, that's what replacement cartilage is for. No zinc for Ernie this time. He was laid up for two months and came out with one leg straight, one bowed. It was another six months before doctors went after the other knee. While he was rehabbing from that realignment—and since they had him sitting still—Ernie's cardiologist souped up his heart with a pacemaker. The warning signs were incidents like his train trip into the Alps and climbing that Mexican pyramid.

"I figured I was stupid, taking two steps at a time," he says of the pyramid.

"They told me, 'Your heart has a murmur in it. If it slows down and stops, it won't start up again.'"   ·

Add it all up, and Ernie spent a decade in the shop. "I don't like it, I'm very unhappy about it," he says. "I'm older, but I'm not feeling that way."

* * *

As winter closed in on the ninety-three-year-old sailor, he readied *Desire* for its winter hibernation. Disconnecting the electricity, swapping out the bolts that hold lines in place in favor of easily removable pins until the mast is taken down for storage. Little things that make pulling his boat from the water go more easily and swiftly.

But now he couldn't get down on the boat's deck and work the wood fittings, sweating the details, as he once did. And on haul-out day, because it was getting difficult for him to clamber around on the boats, he was seeing his role in the crew reduced from what he called the "at large" position to "rover."

"Maybe I'll be transferring some dock lines," he says, accepting his fate. "But for the most part, I spend most of my time sitting on a chair."

He throws up his hands. "I'm older. So what? Live life like you can. Take life as it is. But don't leave it so."

* * *

He cannot leave it so. One morning in 2004, Ernie was going down into basement workshop. He reached for a spot overhead that he always reached for when trying to keep his balance on the steps, and . . .

"I missed," he says. "I actually dove down the steps. I woke up and I thought, what the hell am I doing down here?"

Ernie struggled back upstairs, washed the blood from his forehead, then sat down to recover. Someone came to the door. It was a yachting buddy who was supposed to meet Ernie at the docks so that he could borrow a buffer. When Ernie didn't show, he made the two-minute drive to Ernie's house. Ernie greeted him at the door, still bleeding. Over his protests, he was hustled into the friend's car, a sporty Corvette that felt every dip in the road as they sped to the hospital.

"Every bump we hit, it was, 'Man, oh man!'" Ernie grimaces, reaching for his side at the memory.

"They were more concerned about my head than my ribs," he says. Ernie came through the head examination OK, but those ribs were indeed broken. Four of them, numbers 6, 7, 8, and 9. And it was painful. "You only breathe half a breath for several days," Ernie says.

This would be another extended period of healing. Except this tumble brought about an unexpected result. Going in for the X-rays, Ernie warned the hospital personnel who gathered around, "It'll take a couple of you to get me off this gurney." He was mindful of the pain he'd been in for months and his inability to sit up after lying down since he'd wrecked his back playing that party game in Antigua.

Except now, "no pain," Ernie says, his eyes widening in wonder. The fall down the basement steps completely eliminated the back problem, which never returned.

"They couldn't make anything of it," Ernie says. "My doctor said, 'I wouldn't recommend that as a cure.'"

NINETEEN

Charlie Ross looks back on the twin calamities that preceded Ernie joining his family—his father Gilbert's suicide and the death of Ernie's second wife, Jen—and his judgment is unequivocal. "He saved our family."

Jan Ziobrowski remembers Ernie and Evie as something beautiful.

"That's my favorite love story," she says. "I think everybody was happy about it. It's not like a marriage after a divorce. Both spouses were dead. They were married out of a common need. They needed a mom. We needed a dad. They grew to love each other."

Yet it wasn't a fairy tale. Forging one family from two is a complex, difficult, ongoing process. The kids' ages ranged from married adult to rebellious teen to preschooler. Judy was already married and out of Evie's house. Shirley was seventeen, engaged and almost out: "My mother was against the marriage, let's put it that way," she says.

Charlie was the teenager Ernie remembers as being a difficult kid to talk to. John, a little more than a year behind, took his cues from Charlie. Charlie worked it out just fine, with that thirty-eight-year career at Eastman Kodak, a respected member of the Rochester Yacht Club, cocktails on the lake beneath full sails. John drifted off into heavy drinking, becoming estranged from the family.

And with the two youngest, the same dichotomy. Jan and Patricia were a mere five years old when Ernie and Evie married on April 7, 1961. Jan had her troubles, but she evolved into Ernie's rock. For Pat, it was a life of trouble and, like John, estrangement from the family.

How, given similar circumstances, does one kid take one road while the other wanders off in a completely different direction?

"He took on a lot when he took on our family," Shirley concedes.

And yet, "We just always thought he was amazing," Jan says. "Kind and stern at the same time. Stern, yet fair."

Jan grew into the role of being her stepfather's second in command on board *Desire*, keeping the crews intact for two nights of racing each week, allowing Ernie to simply take the tiller and leave the worries to her as he recovered from his decade of broken femurs and knee replacements.

A lot of healing took place in that family. Bones and spirits. Even Evie's refusal to accept Shirley's husband eased with time. "It worked itself out," Shirley says.

Jan describes Ernie and Evie's union as at first a marriage of convenience. Ernie had built Eileen and Jake's house on Madison Terrace.

"He was always a part of our life," Jan says. Charlie even remembers being in Ernie and Jen's house when he was a little kid. When Ernie and Evie married, no introductions were necessary.

Early in the marriage, Ernie reached out to Evie's kids.

"Before I even knew they were seeing each other, it was my birthday and the phone rang, and here's this guy singing 'Happy Birthday' to me," Judy says.

"We have the same birthday, November 20. Every year, we call each other to sing 'Happy Birthday.' We try to beat each other, see who gets there first. He beat me this year."

The kids testify to their evolving relationships with Ernie, unaware that so many of their words echo each other.

Judy, the oldest: "Oh, my God, he's the greatest. Who comes into a family with four, five kids, and keeps their upbeat attitude? They all took to him as a father."

Shirley, the second oldest: "He was a father figure for the boys and Jan. They were young when Dad died. It was his honesty. He was just a good guy."

Jan, the youngest: "Mom had been the disciplinarian. When Dad came in, the boys were teenagers."

Teenagers. And the young rebels surely would be testing the new guy.

Charlie, the oldest son: "He came in and instilled some discipline into my brother and me. We pretty much had the run of the roost."

With Ernie bringing in his carpenter's paychecks and extra money repairing boats down at the yacht clubs, Evie no longer had to work. Adult supervision increased a few ticks.

"That," Charlie says, "was a positive change in my life.

"I was a bit of a daredevil when I was younger. I would jump off the Elmgrove bridge into the canal. When Ernie heard I was starting to dive off the bridge, he came along and wanted to make sure I was doing it right." Ernie didn't stand on the road shouting instructions or show Charlie a Parks and Recreation department film strip on canal safety. He showed Charlie how to do it by diving off the bridge and into the canal himself.

"Because he had done it as a kid," Charlie says.

Such feats of physical flair are impressive when it's your old man. Charlie remembers being on construction sites when the kids were out of school, watching his ambidextrous stepfather's lunchtime carpentry challenges.

"He could hammer nails with a hammer in each hand," Charlie says. "He'd say, 'Let's see if any of you guys can do this.'"

Years later, Ernie underwent surgery for carpal tunnel syndrome. That's one procedure he forgot to mention while cataloging his replacement parts. Perhaps it's not as interesting as, say, bowel plumbing. Charlie says the doctor told him afterward, "Those are the hardest working hands I've ever had to operate on."

Ernie came about them honestly. He and Evie were Great Depression kids, an experience that was always looking over their shoulders.

"Dad more than Mom," Jan says. "He'd talk about things like how you could buy a loaf of bread for a nickel. But how a nickel was a lot of money."

Again, it's that Greatest Generation ethos we've heard about. Work, Jan says, "is what keeps him going." She shakes her head grimly, the bearer of bad news. "Our generation will never make it. We just don't have the work ethic."

Ernie's generation also played hard. "They were a very socially active couple, Ernie and Evie," Charlie says. "They liked to have a few beers and play cards. They always had a lot of people around them. And they were very good dancers. People liked to watch them dance."

"He read us stories, drew us stick figures," Jan says.

"They had dinner parties, clambakes. He knows you have to grab the gusto when you can. Life is not a dress rehearsal. We could always come to him at any time and talk to him. If he didn't have the answers, he would help me find the answers. He helped me through divorce. A car accident."

Yet Ernie ran out of answers when it came to John. Ernie and Evie had bailed him out of a couple of DWIs.

"They spent a lot of money on him and never felt like they got a proper thank-you," Charlie says.

By the summer of 2010, John was sixty. He'd been estranged from the family for fifteen years and had fled his legal troubles by moving to Florida. Only Jan was staying in touch with him.

"He kept saying, 'I'm not dying; I'm just not feeling great,'" Jan says. Little wonder, the guy was an oncology buffet. "He had three kinds of cancer," Jan says. John died that November.

Nor did Ernie have answers for the path taken by the girl he and Jen had adopted when she was two days old, whom he had taught how to ride a bike and taken for sled rides in the park. Pat Coleman hadn't seen Ernie since his eightieth birthday party, thirteen years earlier. Estranged from the family, she was trapped in Phoenix, living in a home for battered women, unemployed and utterly defeated.

"I should be where Jan is; Jan should be where I am," Pat says. On the phone, her voice sounds weak. She is not in good health. It's her heart, she says.

"I would have, I should have been the one out there crewing on *Desire*."

There is resentment, although little anger. As she tells her story—and it's a wreck of life—Pat knows what went wrong but seems confused as to why. And yet, despite her dire situation, she clings to a sailing memory and a long-distance phone call in a manner that is at once both desperate and endearing.

* * *

It became clear to me that, for better or for worse, Ernie was a man who compartmentalized. He isolated a problem, focused his energy, and came up with a solution. And if the problems were too big to solve, he sailed away from them.

Ernie's most jarring experience with mortality, his final night on *Vincennes*, was not something he talked about.

"No, never," Jan says. "But we can't bury something that long and be rid of it."

No, never. Yet often you can't help but stumble across it. Ernie was the father that Jan remembered, and although Jan knew she'd had another father, she did not know the truth about his death.

"Not right away. I blocked it out," she says.

The family protected the youngest daughter and did not speak of what had happened until she was thirteen. Even then, the details emerged by happenstance. Jan was babysitting for her sister Judy's children.

"The kids knew and they said something about it," Jan says. Her father had shot himself in the woods behind the house.

"I was always told," Jan says, "that he died in a hunting accident."

"It wasn't an easy time," Judy concedes. She was eighteen when her father died.

"Unfortunately, everybody just didn't talk about it. It's one of those things that should have been met head-on."

The unhealthy silence that served as both protection from and denial of Gilbert Ross's death was not an option when Evie grew ill. By 1995, it was clear to all that her health was failing. There was no evading the issue. It had to be dealt with. Ernie did the best he could to ease her way.

"The last day, he called us and said she was going really fast, you need to get down here," Charlie remembers. "That was the only time I ever saw him get mad at her. Well, mad isn't the right word. She wasn't speaking; her breathing was very shallow. Ernie went for a short walk down the street, and that's when she died. He came back and we told him. He just kind of shouted, 'You had to leave me when I wasn't here!'"

It wasn't anger.

"He was a wonderful caretaker, a loving man," Charlie says. "They were a couple in love. It was an inspiration to watch them."

"I used to watch them walking down the street holding hands," Jan says. "Making sure nobody moved Dad's puddle."

Now he was alone again. Just Ernie and his puddle, the lake. Evie's kids watched over him as best they could, but they were spread all over the country. John was in Florida. Judy and her husband Frank Farrand had retired and were living on Oneida Lake, an hour and a half away. Shirley and her husband Elvin—having long ago won Evie's approval— were an hour and a half in the other direction, Horseheads, near Elmira.

Pat had gone into exile in Phoenix. Only Jan and Charlie and his wife Betsey remained in Rochester with Ernie.

"He was miserable," Jan says. "Lonely. He pretty much shut down. We'd do dinner once in a while. But we were all dealing and hurting on our own. We didn't go out of our way like we should have. Mom was the glue that kept the family intact."

This lasted until Marilyn. As he had so many times before, the old carpenter went back to work, rebuilding his life.

"That was a bit of a shock for us," Charlie says. "But it's worked out for Ernie. He's gotten to see the world."

"He asked us, 'Would you rather I sit home alone? Again?'" Jan says. "But traveling, with him and Marilyn, that's been a lifesaver. We all think it's been a great opportunity."

Marilyn's daughter Julie was all for it. She was twenty-five years old at the time, married to a guy eleven years her senior.

"I thought it was a riot," she says of her mother's new boyfriend. "He looked like—what's the name of the guy on the cover of the frozen seafood packages?" A handful of marketing department creations fit that description, Mrs. Paul excluded.

Julie's brother, Steve Lockner, is another late-life addition to Ernie's family tree. He's a bit of a twisted limb, he admits, a garrulous fellow who compares his rough-hewn manner to the Randy Quaid character in the *National Lampoon's Vacation* films.

"I'm the old man with a sailor's mouth who rides a Harley," he says.

But he feels a kinship with Ernie as an ex-military man—Steve was a marine—and as a man who's rebuilt his life as well. Steve is divorced, he lost contact with his first two children, and he acquired two more in a second marriage. Both of them did time as marines as well.

Steve had settled in the rural western New York outpost of Byron, a mechanic, a hands-on man, like Ernie.

"He's an old-school guy, know what I mean?" Steve says. "You can tell a veteran; he has an old-school way of doing things. He doesn't worry about, 'Oh, no, I've got to give the kids a time-out.' He's a proud man, and I'm proud to be his stepson."

He shares his stepsister Jan's bleak view of the future.

"You kind of wish kids nowadays knew half as much as he does about the world," Steve says. "Then you wouldn't worry about them. But they're lazy. Ernie has outlived, what, three wives now? The old guy doesn't stop. And he still has a passion for sailing, even after what happened to him on the *Vincennes*."

It's a steely resilience tempered over nine decades of life. A fourth marriage? Just when his journey was drifting to a stop in the water, Ernie seemed to catch sail-filling breezes. Perhaps it has some connection with what he'd learned on the lake and what Jan says is the best piece of advice that he's shared with her.

"Always know where the wind is."

* * *

The wind carried Pat elsewhere. Everyone seems to hold their breath for a moment when her name comes up.

"You know that Reba McEntire song, 'The Greatest Man I Never Knew'?" Pat says. "That speaks volumes."

The one that goes, "every day we said hello, but never touched at all."

She was Trish to Ernie and Jan; others in the family call her Patti. Patricia is fine, she says. Or better yet, Pat. She doesn't know who she is or where she's going. Once she starts, the story pours out like water from a breached levee.

"I was in an abusive relationship, and I didn't even know it," Pat says. "We had no friends. She was an alcoholic, and she knew how to push my buttons."

Pat explains that she is gay. For a man of Ernie's generation, that can be particularly vexing. What does his life experience tell him about this one?

Pat continues, "We were living at a motel, and after eighteen months we got evicted. So then we're living out of her truck, and I heard about it every day. She was going to get me evicted from her truck. One day we were arguing more than usual. She punched me in the face, broke my glasses."

Pauline, her partner, drove away in her pickup, leaving Pat standing in a parking lot. The two dogs, a Pekingese and a chow, went with Pauline. It's the last time Pat saw any of them.

"I had those dogs since they were puppies," Pat says wistfully. "One was nine and one was ten.

"Since then I've lived in three domestic-violence shelters. Now I'm in a transition shelter for people over fifty. It's supposed to teach you how to be self-reliant.

"At least," she says sardonically, "they don't have all these screaming kids around."

The breakup was a year ago. Where and when did this downward spiral start?

"Jan was the apple of my mother's eye; she could do no wrong, I could do no right," Pat says of Evie. Yet that resentment was erased, she insists, looking back to a day when she was eighteen or nineteen years old. Evie fell off a bicycle and broke an ankle, "and I moved in with her. We were best friends all of a sudden. It turned out she was the most accepting one about me being gay. I think she got to see a side of me she wouldn't have seen otherwise."

Shortly afterward, Pat went off to nursing school. She became an emergency room nurse in Rochester then in Buffalo for twelve years. Ernie and Evie, she says, visited her only twice.

"I'm ninety miles away and nobody comes to see me," Pat says. "I might as well be three thousand miles away."

Perhaps Pat's world was one with which Ernie wasn't comfortable. She and Pauline moved to Phoenix. That's not three thousand miles, but nineteen hundred can feel like enough. Twenty years later, distance hadn't fixed anything. In fact, things got worse. Pat lost her job in 2009.

"I had some problems with the head of nursing," she says. "I surrendered my nursing license voluntarily. A patient accused me of stealing two soda pops from a room. Then the focus became the suicide attempt.

"I felt I was totally alone; I didn't have a job, money." She and Pauline were living in a motel room. They argued more. "I said, 'I could walk out this door and kill myself, and you wouldn't care.' And she said, 'No.' So I took a bunch of pills. Went to a secluded spot, took the pills, and waited for death. I ended up throwing up, massive diarrhea. I made it out to the street and someone with a phone called 911. I was in the hospital a week or ten days, urgent care center.

"Then I went back to the motel."

Pat says she's been born again for years. It doesn't seem to have had the advertised effect.

"I've repented and been baptized. I'm a Christian. I liked the Lutheran church. I tried Pentecostal for a while. That's ten times worse than Baptist.

"I don't think loving somebody is a sin. I've got Jesus and the Lord to help me."

The conversation returns to Pauline.

"I call her Satan. She worked in a floral shop. I got her the job. I saw the 'help wanted' sign in the window and said, 'Why don't you try that place?' Her life was one beer after another, like a chain smoker. When one was empty, she'd go get another one. Twelve, fourteen beers a day. I sure don't miss that 'pop-pop' when you open it. And she would make it louder just because she knew it bugged me.

"I know it will sound pretty sick, but, one of the reasons we stayed together, the dogs were so attached to her. . . ."

A sudden blackness surges through Pat.

"If I had a gun, I'd direct it at my nursing supervisor, my roommate, and then myself."

Seconds later, the darkness passes.

"I'm working on a new career," Pat says. "I was a nurse for thirty-two years. I'm excited about this."

She's taking classes to learn billing, so she can work in a medical office.

"I had to quit half the medication I was on because I couldn't afford it," she says of her heart problems, and she figures office work will take less of a toll on her body than nursing.

"Standing eight and a half hours every day, there's no way I could do that. I'm not even fifty-six years old, and I'm falling apart."

She pauses. "If I had it all over again," she says wistfully, "I would have done things differently."

Differently starting with her life in Rochester.

"When I flew back for my mother's funeral, Dad and I—I think it was the only time—we went out on the boat alone, by ourselves," she says.

"It's like, when you do meditation at the center here, and they tell you, 'Pick one thing that was your happiest moment.' That sail with him, that meant a lot. We were talking about stuff like, he wanted to donate his body to science. I said, 'Wouldn't it be better to be cremated and throw your ashes out on the lake?'

"I had been home a couple of weeks before that to visit my mother before she died. He drove me to the airport, and he was saying, 'When she gets better, we're going to do this, we're going to do that.' And I said, 'Dad, it's too late!' I don't know how much time he thought she had.

"I can't afford to come back," Pat says, now worried about how much time her father had. "I'm just afraid I'm not going to see him again alive."

She resented the attention that Ernie and Evie lavished on other people and their frequent socializing. "It was all about cocktail hours, nightcaps, the morning eye-opener," Pat says.

What Jan calls "typical sibling rivalry" is something that Pat insists runs much deeper. Yet for years, Jan had been the only family member with whom Pat communicated.

After having not spoken to her father in more than a decade, in December 2010 Pat expressed a holiday wish to her sister.

"I told Jan, the one thing I want for Christmas," she says. "'I want Dad to call me.' He did. We didn't get into anything really heavy. But it was like those ten years never happened."

And here the story departs from the Reba McEntire song.

"The first couple of times he called, he missed me. He left a message. He said that he loved me.

"If we never talk again, I saved the message. So I can play it back whenever I want to."

TWENTY

The execution papers were in my briefcase. My father's living will. It called for an end to this nonsense.

Ernie and I had been working steadily on the book when I got the call from my mom. She was at home after spending the night with my father at the hospital. He'd turned off all of the lights in the house and tried to grope his way upstairs in the darkness. Mom always told him to leave the light on when he came up the stairs at night then to turn it off. After all, there was a switch at the top of the stairs. But my father never did anything you told him to do. Stubborn, he'd always do the exact opposite. So leaving himself totally in the dark, as always, he fell down the stairs. It was the night after Christmas, and he was lying on the floor with two broken vertebrae to go with the winter hat and gloves we'd bought him.

It was always difficult to find him just the right thing.

I didn't head back to Cleveland right away. Ernie and I continued to put the book in order. I figured I could be of more use to my dad when he was discharged. His doctors told me a long period of rehabilitation was likely. My brother and I shopped the internet for rehab places for when he was ready to leave the hospital.

That was suspiciously slow in coming. I'd been talking to him by phone since his fall, but after three weeks I wasn't hearing any improvement in his voice. The broken vertebrae had evolved into pneumonia. Then his heart, lungs, kidneys, and bowels began fading. His doctors—he had a half dozen specialists looking after him—would shore up one situation, then another emerged. My father was an old, crumbling dam. He hadn't walked since the night he fell down the stairs. My wife and I decided we'd better make the five-hour drive to Cleveland.

It was a Sunday. About twenty minutes after Margaret and I had arrived at my parents' house, the phone rang. One of my father's lungs had collapsed and his heart stopped. We raced to the hospital. CPR and a defibrillator brought him back, although some ribs were broken getting it done. We waited for hours, then they let us into his room for a few moments. Tubes everywhere. Machines pumping away coldly and efficiently in place of his fading organs. It was moments before he would fade into a drug-induced sleep. The only thing I recognized were his eyes. They looked fierce and perhaps frightened. We all said a few things. My mom leaned over and kissed him. As we left, I turned to look at him one more time. He couldn't speak, but he batted his eyelashes furiously. I think he was telling me he knew it was us.

I didn't know much about this guy, really, even though I'd lived with him for two decades. I'd been told that at Bedford High School he was known for his jitterbugging skills, but I don't think I ever saw him dance. He enlisted in the navy in 1951 for the Korean War and fought on the Key West front for four years. His job was keeping flight logs for the naval air training missions. I suppose this was because he'd won penmanship awards in school. He did have marvelous lettering skills. A precise, mid-century draftsmanship. In fact, after the navy he spent his entire working life first in drafting then as a contracting estimator, working for companies bidding on construction jobs. He'd look at a set of blueprints and compute how many ceiling tiles or how many feet of heating duct would be needed on the site.

I'd been spending a lot of time with Ernie, this average guy caught up in remarkable circumstances. The Great Depression, war, death, healing broken families. I saw that Ernie had not only managed all of this, but he understood how to set it aside when need be and celebrate life. Now I was back in Cleveland, standing over the hospital bed of a complicated guy who'd taught me behaviors that I'd spent my adult life unlearning. I had grown into the classic generational rebel, refashioning myself as the mirror opposite of something that's very difficult to escape.

I knew more about Ernie than I knew about my own father. I knew more funny stories about Ernie. I knew more of life's tragedies that Ernie had faced. I drank more wine with Ernie; I knew more of what Ernie thought about the world.

Ernie was a life force. My father was a vacuum. An empty space, where my father wasn't missing physically but emotionally. He was always right there at 6:15 every evening, silently eating dinner after returning from a job where I had little idea of what he did, before he settled down in front of the television. A guy who I suspect wanted to enjoy his family but didn't know how to do it. A hard, frequently critical, often angry man rarely offering encouragement to his two sons. No, he wasn't missing. But he wasn't available.

My parents had lived in their current house less than ten years. The place had never felt like their home, at least to me. Nothing was familiar, except some old art projects done by my brother and me from our high school days. I'd used colored tissue paper to make a still life of cheap wine bottles. Ripple, Carlo Rossi. They had it hanging on a wall. Hideous.

I saw that my parents had recently bought themselves a couple of early Christmas gifts. One was the "Amish heater" they'd seen advertised on TV. It plugs into the wall and the fake logs glow a cozy orange. An impressionistic fire dances on the back surface. It even gives out a little heat. About five feet away from it, sprawling in the corner of the living room, was their new fifty-five-inch high-definition television. When my father got up in the morning, he'd turn it on, sit in his chair, and stare at Fox News. After a while, maybe he'd strap on his Velcro sneakers and do something, like drive his big riding mower around the lawn in the summer or take the screens out of the windows in the fall. I'm not sure why he insisted on removing the screens. Decades of habit, I guess. A couple of years ago, one spring, we'd even put them in for him. Of course, we'd done it all wrong. You have to wash the windows first, see.

I don't know why. He never seemed to look out the windows much. And the curtains were drawn a lot. That corner of the living room—and now that magnificent new TV—was the center of the universe. It was like a drive-in movie screen, impossible to ignore.

"I feel like I should be sitting in a car while I'm watching this thing," I told my mom.

"Now he's not even going to get to use it," she said.

I wandered around their house, fixing little things. My dad used to take care of stuff like that, unless you told him, "Dad, you ought to take care of that." Then he'd ignore it. But mostly, he was a handyman, until recently. So I tightened up the wobbly kitchen table. The furniture wasn't old, but somehow everything they managed to find was like what they had in the 1960s, all arranged in little conversational groupings for conversations that weren't happening. In the living room were a couple of those comfy chairs that swivel and rock back and forth. Except, when you sat in one of them, it would violently try to dump you, like that scene in one of the early James Bond films in which a displeased Dr. No pushes a button and a henchman sitting at the table gets flipped backward into a tank full of sharks. I turned over the chair and found a hole in the suspension where a bolt was missing. I stuck a new one in there and it worked fine.

One morning I got up at 6 a.m. to take out the garbage, trudging in the snow in the early morning darkness down the 175-yard-long driveway. My mom said I couldn't just leave it out at the end of the driveway the night before because animals would get into it. I think she was right. A few nights earlier I had been awakened by an astonishing cacophony of bloodcurdling howls. Coyotes. My parents were born and raised in the Cleveland suburb of Bedford, but over the years each move had taken them increasingly further from civilization—even that winter home in Florida, in the manicured community of gently curving streets lined with houses with salmon-colored tile roofs. The last time I had visited there—maybe five years earlier—the neighborhood seemed empty. People were dying off or moving into senior living homes. Their kids didn't want to live there, and no one was buying anymore. The electric hedge clippers of the Latino landscaping crews grew silent.

My parents got lucky, selling their Florida place a couple of years earlier. Now they were living in this town far to the southwest of Cleveland. Everyone lived in relatively new houses, clusters of developments ten or fifteen years old, like fearful pioneers circling the wagons, surrounded by acres of land. The people here lived like farmers, but few of them were farming. Every spring, my parents allowed some stranger to drive a tractor through the ten or so acres of their backyard, planting soybeans or corn.

I spent the mornings there sitting at the kitchen table, staring out the back window—the screens were out—watching the dry, broken cornstalks poking up like bleached bones through a few inches of snow and drinking coffee from a mug that read "60: Official Old Fart." That mug was twenty-one years old.

Life with my dad had been a difficult eighty-one years, even though I'd witnessed only fifty-three of them myself. But I'd seen enough. My brother only recently had begun speaking to him after fifteen or so years. I don't know exactly why, but I didn't blame my brother. My dad hadn't been invited to my house since the night he flew into a rage at dinner over some inconsequential and now-forgotten slight, stood up, and pulled his arm back like he was about to hit me. He didn't. He was seventy-one at the time; I suppose even he realized it would have been a ridiculous act. He had never hit me before anyway. Instead, he stormed upstairs and left without a word the next morning, taking my mother with him. That was more like him. My mom called a couple of evenings later and put him on the phone. He apologized, haltingly, but sincerely, I thought. It was the only time in my life that he had ever apologized for anything. I remember that evening well. We were all watching the TV news, images of the Twin Towers falling a few hours earlier.

My father always had been a nougat of crisis wrapped in a layer of tension, but there had never been anything as big as him falling down those stairs. I was feeling some sadness about this, but also a lot of resentment. I was thinking about Ernie, and how his stepkids said that he had saved that family. Yeah, they'd had their problems. The estrangements of Pat and John. Mistakes and misunderstandings are inevitable over the course of nine decades. But I was jealous of families like Ernie's. It took me decades to understand that my dad came from a troubled family and was himself a troubled man, immature and uncomfortable with himself. It wasn't until I was in college around other people that I began to see that. That was the vacuum that Ernie was stepping into for me. I was seeing how responsibility—and being a man—was supposed to work.

On the second and third weeks of his hospitalization, when he often had a tube in his mouth or an oxygen mask, my dad would communicate by writing notes to the nurses. Sometimes the drugs got in the way of his thinking. The nurses showed my brother a note he'd written in some odd code. Something like, "162 square feet versus 120 square feet." At that moment, he must have been drifting through a distant room in his brain that held memories from his estimating days.

* * *

I brought my father's living will along with me on each visit, but I left it in the briefcase. Considering our often difficult relationship, there was something unseemly about me handing over the order of execution to his doctors.

But if not me, who would carry out the assignment? While at my parents' house, I called a few relatives, navigating the dysfunctional family tree. Not everyone actually spoke to each other. I had known this for years, but the disease was more widespread than I'd thought.

One day while sitting next to my father's hospital bed, I noticed a clipboard and a pencil on a table next to him. This must have been what he was using to communicate. I flipped through the blank pieces of paper until I found one with writing that someone had moved to the back of the clipboard. The printing was shaky, but I still recognized my father's penmanship. Three sentences, one an incomplete thought, another asking for something to drink, and the third: "When can I go home?"

He didn't. On Tuesday night, I told my brother about the living will. We all decided, if he wasn't better on Wednesday, I'd show it to his doctors and discuss the options.

Wednesday came. I knew this was the day. There was no improvement. When he came out of sedation, he didn't awaken, as most people did. I told the doctors about my dad's living will—no life support, no life-protracting nutrition—and said it was the family's decision to honor it. At 12:30 p.m., they disconnected him from the equipment. My dad slept through the procedure. An hour later, I suggested to Margaret that she take my mom home; she'd been through enough and didn't want anymore. I sat next to my father, afraid to leave the room.

For the first couple of hours, I thought he looked better than he had in years. Had we made a mistake? He looked comfortable. But then the nurses came in a few times and moved him. I could see how bad he was, withered away. He awoke once as they shifted his position. I stood just behind two nurses, talking to him. He looked past them and straight at me. I think he knew I was there, but his eyes were clouded, a strange gray color. Then the morphine did its work.

A chaplain stuck his head in the door and caught me crying just a little. I said I'd forgiven my dad. I didn't say for what. I'm not even sure for what. The chaplain said it looked like something important was happening here.

I sat next to my dad for eight and a half hours, most of the time just watching him breathe. I didn't think it was possible to sit like that for so long and do nothing. His signs were steady, and by 9 p.m., I decided to leave.

At midnight, the nurse called from the hospital. The numbers on all of that equipment surrounding him were fading. I sat in the dark for a few moments and decided against waking my mom. I wasn't going to go, I was going to go, I wasn't going to go. . . . Twenty minutes later, the phone rang again. He was gone.

* * *

My mom handled it well. She referred to him in the present tense most of the time, but she understood. The first night after my dad died, we were watching an old Peter Sellers comedy on the fifty-five-inch TV when, out of nowhere, she said, "I wonder how long it takes to burn a body?"

Her husband was being cremated. She decided to delay a funeral and memorial service until later—a later that didn't happen at all. That was my father's choice as well. I made the phone calls, my brother and I put together a card bearing the news to others. We wrote an obituary for the newspaper. But for the most part, it was almost as if my dad had just simply vanished.

Margaret and I drove back to Rochester. And Ernie and I went back to work.

TWENTY-ONE

The folk singer Joan Baez had been in town a few weeks earlier. That got Ernie to talking of the 1960s and the Vietnam War.

"They really gave her trouble over that," he says of Baez's antiwar activism. But that was more than four decades ago, and things look a little different now.

"I think we should have kept our noses out of it," he says. "She was right."

Ernie would lapse into the language of his era, sometimes calling the Pacific campaign of World War II the "Jap war." Language and ideas that lingered from December 1941, when he was still a stateside civilian and *Life* magazine was offering its readers a guide about how to identify enemy aircraft that might attack the United States.

And a story on "How to Tell Japs from the Chinese." If Ernie read that story, he would have learned that "physical anthropologists" are "devoted debunkers of race myths." Yet in the name of homeland security, *Life* nevertheless plunges into race myths: Chinese are tall and slender, Japanese short and squat.

I was never sure if Ernie had strong political leanings, even on the rare occasion when he said something that seemed to have been lifted from conservative TV talk shows, like Iranians not valuing life. Words that aren't surprising when they come from older Americans, who tend to lean conservative and slightly more nationalistic, if I may venture into the territory of ageist myths. Yet Ernie also could drift to the left. After two stints in the navy, he was no hawk.

"I think the United States is flexing its muscles too much," Ernie says. "We've got one hell of a mess in Afghanistan and Iraq."

It's 2011 and he's sitting in his kitchen on a beautiful fall morning in Rochester. After a little more than a year of work, the book is almost done. The leaves, now brown, are slowly dropping from the tulip tree. They are huge, bigger than my hand when I spread my fingers wide. At the end of his street, Lake Ontario is a steely, misty gray. Later in the week, Ernie will be taking *Desire* out of the water and putting it away for the winter. A sailing season is gone yet again, for the thirty-eighth time with *Desire*. It feels like a reflective morning.

Q: You've enjoyed a good, long, healthy life. How did that happen?

A: "I never worried about anything. I never was the kind of guy, when I had a headache, who took an aspirin. Now I'm pumping fifteen pills a day. I've had a few tragedies, my wives dying. In my late fifties, I told myself, 'If I die tomorrow, I haven't missed anything.'"

Q: What's the most important thing you've ever done?

A: "When I married Evie, she had five kids, I had a little girl. Yeah, I would say that's the most important thing. I helped mold the kids. I feel the parent is responsible for a lot of the bad habits. Of course, you can't hit them anymore. I say, 'Spare the rod, spoil the child.' I never regretted a moment. Now my son Charlie says, 'If Dad's happy, that's all that matters.' Jan and Marilyn gang up on me."

Ernie describes how, earlier in the summer, a growth had reappeared on his left cheek. He put off taking care of the problem. Their insistence that he see a doctor was simply nagging. But it was removed and, yes, it was cancerous.

"They were asking me, 'Did you go see the dermatologist yet? Did you go see the dermatologist yet?'" Ernie waves his hand dismissively and says of Jan, "You'd think she was my own child. She loves to sail. She loves to maintain a boat."

Q: Do you read much?

A: "No. I read magazines. Sailing magazines. I read them from stem to stern. I read short stories. I always take a book on trips." Ernie shuffles into the living room and returns with two John Grisham paperbacks, *The Last Juror* and *The Broker*. "I like the O'Brien books. I've read all twenty of them." That's Patrick O'Brien, author of a series of naval adventures set during the Napoleonic Wars.

Q: So you do read?

A: "If I read for half an hour, I fall asleep."

Q: Ever been in a bar fight?

A: "No. Never. I've had a few fights but not in bars. I almost killed a marine once, then I got pulled off. I would have killed the son of a bitch." I can't let this story get away. While based in Maui, Ernie had been "palling around," as he calls it, with a member of WAVES, or Women Accepted for Volunteer Emergency Service, the female division of the navy. So while married to Ruth, the once girl-shy Ernie had found himself a girlfriend, before Jen even. He recalls one night trying to get into a dance, but he didn't have his ID card on him. The marine at the door turned them away. In Ernie's estimation, the guy was being a jerk.

The next day, Ernie and his WAVE pal were at the beach when he spotted his surly foil from the night before in the water. Ernie swam up to him. "I could hold my breath for over a minute underwater," Ernie says. "I said to him, 'I remember you, you were the SOB who wouldn't let me in the dance the other night.' I stuck my head under the water and hit him in the gut with my head. That's one thing I eventually got over: when I got mad I would see red. I pulled him under the water. I would have drowned him, but a couple of my buddies ran into the water and pulled me off. The strangest thing is, I became good friends with him."

That about-face came when Ernie drove a truckload of plywood up to Haleakala volcano and the Fourth Marine Division's camp to use as flooring for the marines' tents after rainstorms. Ernie's antagonist was now the sentry who waved Ernie and his truck through the gate. They recognized each other. Getting a man out of the mud heals a lot of wounds.

Q: Ever meet a celebrity?

A: "Ted Turner." That's when the TV mogul and former America's Cup sailor was at the Rochester Yacht Club in 1998 for the Ted Turner Great Eight Match Races. There have been other brushes with fame.

"I saw Clark Gable in LA, almost a handshake away. I was very impressed with him. He was a man's man, a ladies' man. That voice of his was something else. Dorothy Lamour. I was really surprised at how small she was. She didn't have any makeup on; I hardly recognized her. It was a crowd situation. Makeup is a wonderful thing for women." He pauses for a half second. "And men!"

Q: What's your all-time favorite movie?

A: "I think I was quite impressed with *Wings*. There were no women in it. It was strictly an airplane war." Ernie's talking about the 1927 silent film about World War I dogfights, although he evidently forgot that Clara Bow had a major role. Of course, he was a kid then; his brain probably wasn't picking up on the romantic junk. Ernie was in high school when he saw the 1931 version of *Dracula*. "The one that scared me the most was that vampire movie. Bela Lugosi. I ran home in the middle of the street, I was so scared. And I lived a mile from the theater."

Q: What's the most beautiful place you've ever been?

A: "To me, I guess it's Lake Ontario. I've seen all of the shores of Lake Ontario, and I find a lot of beauty in that. I was very impressed with the Canadian Rockies, too. Marilyn did the driving; I just watched. They're so different than the American Rockies. Every turn we made was a different rock formation."

Q: What's it feel like to be at the helm of *Royal Clipper*?

A: "Dreams come true. The thrill of all thrills. Especially putting it through maneuvers. Tacking and jibing. Here I am in charge of this five-thousand tonnie."

Q: During the Cold War, did you think the Russians were going to drop an atomic bomb on us?

A: "No. No, no, no. I think they realized we had a few we could drop on them. I worry about Iran, the way they don't value life. They could drop some bombs on Israel, wipe them out. Then they get wiped out. But they don't care; they don't value life at all."

Q: What was your favorite car?

A: "The one I have now. It's a luxury car. It's got everything on it. It drives so beautiful. There's only one problem: it goes faster than it should. You can be doing fifty and you don't realize it, eighty and you don't realize it." Apparently he's referring to the white 2000 Buick LeSabre parked in the driveway. I feel a little let down by that answer.

Q: How about something cooler?

A: "Hudson Terraplane, 1937 convertible. It had an electronic shift. It had this little thing on the wheel, and you pushed it, but it didn't shift until you put the clutch in." This little gadget was known as the Electric Hand.

"That was a fast car," Ernie says. "We had drag races in East Rochester. I beat everybody because of that automatic shifter."

Q: You've played a lot of bridge. What's the secret?

A: "The secret is remembering what's been played. And also have a partner who understands the bidding. That's in—what do you call it?—duplicate bridge. I haven't played bridge in thirteen years."

Q: You've said you were happy to break 100 playing golf. What have you learned from the game?

A: "It's good exercise. If I hit a bad shot, I say, 'Oh, I've got another chance at it.' If I hit a good shot, 'Wow, I did that?'"

Q: What is your most unusual talent?

A: "Ambidextrous? I played tennis with no backhand, just shifting the racket. When I use a hammer, whichever hand picks it up does the work. Saw, same thing. Either hand. I write left-handed. Shoot pool, shuffle cards, left hand. Kick a football, right foot." Ambidexterity came about after Ernie caught his right hand in a door when he was six years old, nearly severing two fingers. "I couldn't use them when I was learning how to write, so the teacher had me write with my left hand. Until that, I was right-handed."

Q: What was your best year ever?

A: "Best year sailing? Golf? Bowling? One year I won everything with Roger and Diane." Those are two longtime crewmates on *Desire*, Roger and Diane Libby. Ernie wanders off into the hall and returns with a silver plate, first place in the under-thirty-foot class. It's from a Scotch Bonnet Race in 1994, sailing across Lake Ontario, rounding Scotch Bonnet Island, then back home.

"That year I won the Freeman, which is a long-distance race. I won the fleet championship at the Rochester Yacht Club in my division. Fleet champion at Genesee Yacht Club in my division. The Oak Orchard Race, the Rochester race. I think it was seven first places, where I got yellow flags. Gold flags, they call them. The Freeman Cup was on a Wednesday. Sail to Sodus, then Ford Shoals, ten miles east of Sodus. Round that mark, sail to Braddock Bay. Round that mark, sail to Rochester. A forty-mile spinnaker run. It was gorgeous."

Q: Do you think there is life on other planets?

A: "The latest news, it's possible. I think it's possible."

Q: Why do you like to dance?

A: "I love flowing with the music. Especially the waltzes. Fox-trots. Rumbas. Salsas. I used to do them all. I loved to jitterbug. Evie and I used to cut some good rugs. She was a wonderful dancer. I did the cha-cha." Ernie begins to sing: "Tea for two, two for tea. . . ."

Q: If you had never seen a sailboat, what do you think you would have done with your life?

A: "It's hard to imagine. Hard to imagine. In other words, I never gave it a thought."

Q: You always seem to know a lot about the things around you. The history, the geography, how stuff was made. How important is that?

A: "I have a very inquisitive mind. When I was a kid and I had toys, I used to take them apart and see what made them click. I always try to fix everything. I always like to know why and how."

Q: You've been involved in two wars, watched a few others. Is it worth it?

A: "You've got me wondering on that. In this Iraq thing, we didn't go far enough in the first place."

He's talking about George H. W. Bush's 1991 Gulf War.

"We should have completed that job. Bush got chicken on that. By the same token, I don't think Iraq will ever become one nation. It's been three nations forever. To combine three nations will not be easy. The Kurds have been the most successful, although they have a problem with Turkey. The Jap war, that was necessary, that was invasion, that's what brought America together again. Unfortunately, it didn't end wars; it wasn't the war to end all wars. There will always be war. In my lifetime, anyway."

TWENTY-TWO

In the fall of 2012, diesel-belching heavy equipment—bulldozers, excavators, front-end loaders, dump trucks—ripped into a weary looking, block-long parking lot in downtown Rochester. The asphalt was broken up and peeled away, the machines scraping and clawing and sweeping away broken brick and debris, revealing the remains of the old RKO Palace Theatre. Forgotten for more than four decades, the theater looked much like the foundations of a forgotten civilization rescued by a team of archaeologists. A vast hole, which was once the huge lobby, the largest of any of the old downtown theaters, leading to the sloped floor and its terraced steps, where thirty-two hundred chairs once were lined in gently curving rows. What had been lost was clear to see again.

Built in 1928 and originally called the Keith Albee Palace Theater, the decor was elaborate, from the marble floors with their Persian rugs to the huge, winding staircase. A great Wurlitzer organ rose from the floor on an elevator.

"Panels of gold satin brocades are outlined with low-relief decoration in ivory, gold and silver," the *Democrat and Chronicle* wrote at the time, "with the entrances to the men's and women's lounge rooms at the right hung with heavy gold draperies. Four large crystal chandeliers are suspended from this dome ceiling with smaller torchiers along the walls."

The Ink Spots performed here. Big-band singer Vaughn Monroe. Amos 'n' Andy. Eddie Cantor. Edgar Bergen. Bob Hope. Ethel Waters. Fred Waring and his Pennsylvanians. George Burns and Gracie Allen. Kate Smith. Paul Whiteman and his orchestra. The Fourteen Bricktops, a jazz band of red-haired women. Rin Tin Tin had a weeklong run, performing tricks. Rose's Twenty-five Midgets, vaudevillians ranging from nineteen to forty-four inches tall.

Movies were shown here as well, always preceded by a handful of cartoons. When the first CinemaScope film, *The Robe*, came to town in 1953, surplus army searchlights were positioned outside, sweeping the skies to announce the event.

The Palace fell to the wrecking ball in 1965. Watching the heavy equipment working over the site, chewing at the foundation, it was now little more than a gravel pit that would soon evolve into a bus station. A necessity, perhaps, and also a reminder that society no longer aims to build on a grand scale. The RKO was architecture as an event. It made coming downtown seem like a wondrous evening. Ernie was there many times, he told me.

I never saw it except through his eyes.

* * *

Throughout the twentieth century, marvelous, poignant, funny, tragic things happened right in front of Ernie, even if he didn't know it at the time. Like the day some guys down at the docks offered Ernie and a couple of his teenage buddies a ride out into Lake Ontario on their big motor launch. This was the early 1930s, the country was sagging beneath the Great Depression, and this kind of offer didn't come by often. They rode to the middle of the lake, where the launch met another boat. The two crews quickly transferred a big load of boxes wrapped in bulky sacks onto the boat Ernie and his pals were riding. Then they returned to shore, the men on the launch encouraging Ernie and his friends to wave as they passed the coast guard station at the mouth of the Genesee River, before puttering past it and tying up at the docks. Nothing to see here, just a little joyride. As Ernie walked away, he saw the mysterious sacks being loaded discreetly onto a waiting truck.

"They told me to not say anything about it," Ernie says. "So I didn't."

Decades later, Ernie figured it out. It was during Prohibition. The launch owners were bootleggers. Ernie and the boys had helped provide cover for a shipment of illegal booze from Canada.

That's typical of Ernie. Every day with him, another story emerges. "Didn't I tell you that one?" he says in amazement.

No. What else have we missed?

Now I'm driving, Ernie's riding shotgun as he conducts a leisurely auto tour of his life. This will take all afternoon. No matter. "I don't keep track of time anymore," he says.

The tour starts in East Rochester, along Commercial Street, through the heart of downtown. After the death of his father, George Coleman, Ernie moved here to an apartment with his mother and her new husband, Alfred Kyle. It was on Commercial Street that Ernie—he must have been five or six at the time—stopped an electric trolley car by standing on the tracks and, with a handful of pennies, demanded to be taken to visit his grandmother.

Turn right on Grant Street. The street names are very American, named for presidents or trees. The house Ernie lived in as a teenager looks different now, he says. It's a typical small two-story home of the era. The front porch has been enclosed since he moved, like a hand held over the eyes, no longer a space in which to hang out on a summer day and shout to neighbors passing by.

"I used to like to sit there and watch the storms come in from the west," Ernie says.

"That two-car garage back there, I helped build that. I built my first boat in there."

His stepfather, a lightweight navy boxing champ, taught Ernie how to fight in that backyard. The two were close, and Ernie respected the toughness of this navy fireman, stoking the ship's boilers.

"As a fireman, you had to be rugged," Ernie says.

That rugged nature grew out of family matters and a house full of Kyle boys.

"They fought among each other when they were growing up," Ernie says. "But if you messed with one of them, they stuck together. They had a lot of respect in this town."

Grant Street was Ernie's home throughout his high school years and then during his mother's illness and death from cancer. He brought his first wife, Ruth, to live there before moving to Marion Street. Alfred, with the Grant Street house to himself, later remarried.

"He couldn't stand being alone," Ernie says, an echo of his own words following the deaths of his second and third wives. Ernie's mother is buried in the Coleman family plot in a cemetery not far from the Grant Street home alongside her first husband. Alfred is in another cemetery, buried next to his second wife.

Ernie will allow for no such confusion when he goes.

"I'm gonna be powder off the side of the boat," he says. "Three buddies are there already."

That had been Pat's suggestion: cremation, with his ashes scattered in the lake.

On the way out of East Rochester, Ernie points out the high school built on the site of the old school he once attended. The middle school is next door.

"They put in a pool," he says, nodding at the outdoor addition. "Our pool was Irondequoit Creek."

It's a ten-minute ride to Rochester and the house on Marion Street. Another two-story residence, it's no longer the duplex that Ernie, his brother Frank, and their wives shared.

"That lot goes way back," Ernie says, pointing around the side of the house.

"We had a victory garden out back. That garage is new. And the house had two doors in front, one to the upstairs apartment, one downstairs. Wow, it is different."

Gleason Works, the gear manufacturing plant at which Ernie worked, is nearby. The neighborhood's built up now with the detritus of fast-food commerce: KFC, Tim Hortons.

"America is different than Europe," Ernie says. "They don't tear things down in Europe."

He points to a tall, battered old roof crowded out of the picture by newer buildings in front of it.

"They made ammunition there during World War I," he says. Artillery shells.

That building appears empty. Gleason Works is still active, and although its mission has not changed, the gears it grinds are no longer for cannons and tanks but for trucks. But there's not as much call for precision American gears these days. A section of the building has been rented to the George Eastman Museum as a vault to store film and photographs of historical value in a cool, dry environment.

By the time he'd left Gleason Works, joined the navy, and returned in one piece, Ernie's idea of what he'd do with his life was evolving. His passion was building things—the cottage on Canandaigua Lake, the garage on Grant Street, his first boat, coffins for navy fliers who'd misjudged the distance to a mountain. We sat in the car in the parking lot at Gleason

Works as laborers began leaving for the day. Ernie recalled how, after returning from the war in 1945, he'd turned his back on such hot, indoor shift work in favor of working outdoors in construction—and repairing boats at the yacht clubs.

Ernie preferred being his own man, but temptation came his way. A salesman from 3M, the chemical company, brought Ernie a compound that had been used to seal wood joints on aircraft carrier decks in the sweltering South Pacific, suggesting he try it on the yachts he was refitting. Ernie used the goop on seven boats, and both he and 3M were satisfied.

"They offered me $10,000 a year, plus expenses and commissions, to sell the stuff," Ernie says. Pretty good money in that day.

"I would have been going up and down the coast, as weather permits, and demonstrating this stuff. I turned it down."

We drove on to the first home he had owned on Titus Avenue in the suburb of Irondequoit. I pull over to the side of the road so we can inspect it. Ernie lived here with Ruth. It is immaculate and well landscaped.

"Boy, did they change it," he says, impressed. "I planted those trees, by the way," he adds, pointing out two hefty cedars in the front yard. The house has acquired an addition, the second floor now extending over the garage roof.

"I built my last boat in that garage, right under those bay windows," he says. Ernie was sailing with the Newport Yacht Club on Irondequoit Bay at the time, and he was the toast of the coast. Those regattas often ended at his driveway.

"My house looked like a flophouse," he says. "Everybody brought sleeping bags and just threw them on the floor. We had so much damn fun."

But things change, as Ernie keeps saying throughout the drive. Although Lake Ontario was once visible from the front yard of this house, it's now obscured by tall trees. And this was where his marriage crumbled. This was where he'd told Ruth he wanted a divorce and left her with everything except his tools, his clothes, and his last Snipe, *Feather*. The navy summoned Ernie again, he remarried, Ruth remarried, and she died after falling down the stairs in this house. Several families have probably since passed through here; as our car pulls away, the front door opens and a black teenager steps outside.

Then we cross the river into the western suburb of Greece. Ernie has never been to CM Gifts and Militaria. I'd been careful to keep our conversation away from *Vincennes* and Savo Island all these months but have decided to take a chance here. Perhaps this visit will pry loose something new from Ernie.

It's a tiny store specializing in combat-ready M-16 bayonets, division coffee mugs, canteens, gas masks, and $121 sand-colored desert boots built to specs by the U.S. Army's official supplier. History is here. One wall is decorated with newspaper stories, obituaries, photos, and certificates honoring Medal of Honor winners with local connections. On one crowded wall is an old newspaper photo of a ship that looks quite similar to *Vincennes*. It is *Philadelphia*, the class of cruisers built after *Vincennes*.

The store's owner, Charles Rabidoux, has been around all kinds of veterans. The ones who talk. The ones who don't. He sometimes offers them advice about how to go about collecting benefits or whom to see about medical or psychological issues. Rabidoux has a calm, encouraging manner about him.

Ernie putters around.

"This is interesting," he says quietly, the well-stocked shelves a wave of distant memories, before being directed to a glass case filled with medals, mostly brass, affixed to bright ribbons. The military industrial complex and assorted manufacturers of reproductions produce an astounding number of tchotchkes. Rabidoux patiently explains what some of them represent. A medal for those who completed training in the United States and were subsequently sent overseas. A medal celebrating the World War II victory. Here, one awarded to anyone who served in the South Pacific naval campaign.

Ernie nods. "I had some of these, but I didn't hang on to them," he says.

He points to another medal, one with a purple ribbon and a heart shape enclosing a bronze portrait of George Washington.

"Of course, I had one of those."

The Purple Heart. For servicemen wounded in action. Ernie never had mentioned it.

The driving tour of Ernie's life moves on toward the lake and a mere three weeks of his life, a period after he'd quit Gleason Works but before he joined the navy. The Odenbach shipbuilding plant is a massive shed visible from a long distance over the treetops. Ernie was a machinist here when Odenbach was building 180-foot-long, shallow-draft oil tankers called lighters. Alongside the building sits Round Pond, which received the finished ships.

"We'd stand over there and watch them plop into the water," Ernie says. "One every eight days."

The new ships would be floated along Round Pond and an accompanying channel until they reached Edgemere Drive, which runs parallel to the beach. The channel cut through the road, flowing beneath a bridge. When a tanker with its thirty-foot beam had to pass through, pontoons below the bridge were filled with air, raising the bridge and allowing the ship to be pushed out of the way. The ship continued into Lake Ontario, up the St. Lawrence River to the Atlantic Ocean and to the war.

Odenbach was tough work, tough on a man's health. Ernie recalls how the building filled with smoke from welding equipment. Now the building is silent, a fragile cavern of iron ribs, sheet metal, and broken glass, like an impossibly large and abandoned cicada shell lying in a meadow surrounded by well-rutted gravel parking lots.

"It's amazing it's stood this long," Ernie says.

The tour resumes, following the lake toward the Rochester Yacht Club. Past the closed Russell power station with its twin smokestacks, each 250 feet tall. Seen from out on the lake, they were the most prominent aspect of the shoreline. Ernie undoubtedly won many races by watching these stacks, the drift of the smoke informing him of the wind direction. He says the builder of this sixty-three-year-old relic was a sailor as well, one who insisted that the stacks line up precisely north-south so that boats on the lake could check their compasses against them.

Ernie knows this kind of stuff. Not many people do. Today, sailors use a global positioning system. Some of what Ernie learned over the years may seem quaint—like how he repaired the rust holes on his old yellow van by covering them with sheet metal held in place by pop rivets—but it worked.

At the lake, his natural habitat, Ernie settles in at the Rochester Yacht Club bar and orders a glass of merlot.

"This is my project every year," he says, running his hands along the shiny, mahogany-red wood, heavily varnished. "I've got fourteen coats on it now."

The clubhouse itself is comfortable elegance, although Ernie laments that this wood is only a thin veneer. He must be careful as he sands it for next year's coat, lest he grind through to the rougher wood below.

Perched on his stool like a hobbit, Ernie chats with the women bartenders. They know him. Everyone seems to know Ernie, although he insists he's not in there often. But he understands this environment. "I cut my teeth on the yacht clubs of the thirties," he says. Back then he helped build the Newport Yacht Club, maybe a mile away, overlooking Irondequoit Bay. Build, literally. The club had eighteen members, and each sacrificed a week's pay to buy the materials. "I was making $15 a week," Ernie says, so it was no palace. "We built it, did the painting, searched for the materials. We made a club out of it." The nearby Genesee Yacht Club, which he belongs to now, as well, is the same rec room environment.

A few stray thoughts and the glass of wine catch up with Ernie after these ruminations on his life. He'd been to seven funerals in the past year, with another on the schedule. The subject of his daughter Pat—the one in so much trouble in Arizona—comes up.

"She was always getting involved with losers," he says sadly. "There's nothing I can do."

He dwells on his acquired family.

"Heartaches and headaches, but I loved it with a passion."

It's a series of complex relationships amplified by his own long life. His oldest daughter, Judy, is three years older than his wife, Marilyn.

Ernie looks out the big windows to the far side of the river and sees the terminal where, a few years ago, the city's fast ferry would tie up. Ferries had been a part of Ernie's Rochester throughout his early years. For his senior class day, seventy-five of his fellow classmates at East Rochester High School rode the streetcar into Rochester, all the way up Lake Avenue, where they caught the ferry across the lake to Cobourg. Leaving at 7 in the morning, they were home by midnight.

"It only cost me $3.25," Ernie says.

Seventy years later, Rochester's new fast ferry debuted in 2004, a part of the declining city's hopes for revival. It would now cost $37, one way, for a trip to Toronto. It was a beautiful ship but financially unworkable and out of business after two summers. Three years later it was sold to a German company. As we sat looking at its old pier, that ferry was churning its way through the channel between Spain and Morocco.

Ernie had never bothered to ride it. "Now, it's so easy to get to Toronto by car," he says. "And it's quicker, really." Speed and convenience have overtaken the more measured ways of his youth.

As Ernie nurses his glass of wine, he dwells on more change. He was once fascinated by flying. He remembers as a kid seeing a Curtiss Jenny biplane, built seventy-some miles away in Hammondsport, rumbling low over East Rochester. He chased it down the streets and through the fields to the now-extinct Brizee Field—Jennies could fly remarkably slow—to watch it land.

This was the beginning of Ernie's youthful dalliance with flight.

"All I knew was the Wright brothers before that," he says. "I was going to be a pilot, no question."

Airplanes were still an uncertain commercial enterprise then, mainly working as mail planes and generally seen as more of an adventurous amusement than something that could change the world.

"Then they built 'em big enough to carry passengers," Ernie says. "But they thought jet planes wouldn't make it. All of a sudden they realized, you get there quicker and carry more people."

Ernie's remembrances often had a beautiful naïveté. Dashing through meadows as a kid while a Jenny soars overhead. Back then, the pilot would take you up for a dollar a ride. Entrepreneurs that they were, Ernie and his buddies worked a deal where they'd wash the planes for a free flight. Forget jumping off the canal locks. Flying was the new frontier, the new thrill. Seeing the massive dirigibles of the day—*Hindenburg*, *Shenandoah*, and *Macon*—silently passing over Rochester during his youth further stoked that interest.

But Ernie's romanticism always has been balanced by reality. *Hindenburg*, *Shenandoah*, and *Macon* all came to newspaper headline endings. His romance with the air, and perhaps the securing of his partnership with the water, cooled at Brizee, as well, with another landing, if it can be called that.

"He was coming in. He didn't make it," Ernie recalls.

The plane wrecked in a creek bed.

"They go 'splat' when they hit," Ernie says. "I didn't see the crash, but I saw them taking out the body. Looked like a bowl of jelly. I didn't go back there. That turned me off."

The day's tour of Ernie's life is nearly over. He's looking out the window at the river shimmering in the late afternoon sun. I think about asking him about that last night on *Vincennes* now. But I can't bring myself to do it, can't disrupt the afternoon of this ninety-four-year-old man and his glass of wine. Instead I hand him something I'd quietly purchased at CM Gifts and Militaria while he was looking elsewhere. The medal awarded to anyone who served in the South Pacific naval campaign.

"I want you to have this," I said. "You earned it."

"You didn't have to do that," Ernie says. He looks at the medal for a moment—it has the silhouette of a warship—then quietly slips it into his shirt pocket. He doesn't let on what he makes of it. Maybe nothing, as he has for seventy years. Maybe something. Because I know he thinks about it, perhaps fleetingly. He displays his sailing trophies prominently. His medals from World War II are lost in a drawer somewhere, I suppose, if he even still has them.

We finish our wine. Good stories, but I had hoped for more on this drive. The revelation about his Purple Heart is the best that I will get. In this last official interview for the book, the last chance to see if Ernie volunteers something on the missing piece, *Vincennes*, he remains silent.

TWENTY-THREE

A muggy and extraordinarily dark evening smothered the southwestern Pacific Solomons. No moon illuminated the waters around Guadalcanal Island and its accompanying string of islands, including Florida and Tulagi, with its golf course and cricket club built by the British as a way of dragging Western civilization to this part of the world.

And, just to the north of Guadalcanal, Savo Island.

For two days, *Vincennes*, its sister ships *Astoria* and *Quincy*, and the Australian cruiser *Canberra* had been covering the landings of the marines on Guadalcanal and Tulagi, lobbing eight- and five-inch shells at the islands and swatting at the Japanese fighter planes, dive-bombers, and torpedo bombers arriving to challenge the invaders. The Imperial Japanese Navy, despite reports of its presence in the area, had yet to make an appearance.

On this, the evening of August 8, 1942, combined fleet commander Rear Admiral Victor Crutchley had a handful of warships at his disposal. Six heavy cruisers, two light cruisers, fifteen destroyers, and five minesweepers. Crutchley divided this force in half. One group to watch the southern approach to the islands, the second group to patrol the north.

The plan did not work. Incredibly, seven Japanese cruisers and one destroyer entered New Georgia Sound under cover of darkness virtually undetected, the few warnings of their presence ignored. In a short, brutal battle that lasted little more than thirty minutes, four Allied cruisers sailed into the fog of war. For weeks, it was as though they had never existed.

In Ernie's home city of Rochester, for four cents a day, the *Democrat and Chronicle* slowly, ever so slowly—and as best as the wartime censors would allow—broke the news to the folks back home. The war, heavily edited, unfolded in thick, black headlines:

BATTLE STILL RAGES IN SOLOMONS

"Jap Resistance Is Considerable, Navy Discloses," the subhead announced on August 10 in the first of the Associated Press stories from the scene:

> Competent British circles dismissed the Japanese claim of sinking or damaging 28 vessels in the Solomon Islands battle yesterday and suggested that the enemy, as in the past, was making sweeping victory assertions to prepare the Japanese people for bad news of their own losses
>
> Flamboyant Japanese broadcasts that 11 transports and 17 other "Anglo-American" warships were damaged suggested that the great naval battle was covering an invasion to drive the enemy from the southern Solomons, 900 miles northeast of Australia.

On the following day, "Disclosing this late yesterday afternoon," the AP reported that

> the Navy revealed that the furious assault, in which the Marines were strongly backed by warships and planes, had already cost the United States forces at least one cruiser sunk and two damaged and two destroyers and one transport also damaged.
>
> The Japanese, whose counterattack was launched "with rapidity and vigor," have suffered a "large number" of surface units destroyed and put out of action, the Navy statement said.
>
> The Navy statement warned that "considerable losses" must be expected.

Two days later, "details of the naval battle are 'not yet available,'" the *Democrat and Chronicle* told its readers. And other fights demanded attention. The Japanese were in Alaska's Aleutian Islands and were invading New Guinea.

Meanwhile, in Europe:

GERMANS SMASH NEARER TO STALINGRAD

A curiosity from newspapers of the day was the practice of running delayed dispatches, reporters' stories often held up for weeks until approved by the wartime censors. On an inside page of the August 17 *Democrat and Chronicle* was one such story that, despite the absence of details such as ship names and locations, appears to have been filed from *Vincennes*'s squadron after it left Pearl Harbor.

> This American naval force, bound for "somewhere," gave an impressive preview of things to come today in a slashing, thunderous drill with live ammunition which was marked by the fine timing of a crack football team.
>
> Orange flames spurted from the muzzles, which were enveloped in thick shrouds of coal-black smoke seconds later as the guns settled back into their sockets. Huge white puffs rose from the tiny uninhabited island where the projectiles crashed and exploded.
>
> It was all over in what seemed like a few minutes.

A sentence that eerily foreshadowed the battle that was to come.

Ten days after *Vincennes* and its fellow cruisers had engaged the Japanese at Savo Island, the news reports recycled U.S. Navy claims:

NAVY CLAIMS SEA VICTORY OFF ISLAND

A secondary headline carried the caveat "Spokesman Warns Victory Cost U.S. Losses." As the story noted, "The Navy carefully refrained from announcing the extent of damage to American forces, saying that such information would be of value to the enemy—but it had previously announced that one U.S. cruiser had been sunk and two cruisers, two destroyers and one transport damaged."

Truth closed in two days later in an official statement from Australia. "Prime minister John Curtain today announced the loss of the Australian cruiser *Canberra* in the Solomon Islands battle." The statement promised "few casualties." Small comfort to the families of the eighty-four men who died on that ship.

By August 21, news reports announced that the U.S. Marines were "mopping up" on Guadalcanal, and a day later, the big black headlines announced:

JAP FORCE IN SOLOMONS WIPED OUT

It was almost too easy to believe. News reports on August 23 informed readers back home in Rochester that "Marines Force Japs to Pay at 27-to-1 Ratio in Solomons." Official word from the front arrived via one of the delayed dispatches, in which a reporter returning from the battle reported all was well, with no mention of the early morning hours of August 9 off Savo Island.

Stalingrad was still front-page news. The battles raged on in New Guinea and the Aleutian Islands. And battles raged in courtrooms as well. Comedian Georgie Jessel's wife had been granted a divorce after two years of marriage. She had been only sixteen when they'd married, but she now realized that the forty-four-year-old Jessel was "too old for me and I am too young for him."

And there was this to worry about now:

ROMMEL ATTACK IN EGYPT DESERT

On September 4, the newspaper's front page featured a large photo of a returning U.S. Navy warrior accompanied by a few sentences summarizing his estimate of the Guadalcanal campaign action.

> First Lieutenant-Commander George Huff, first Navy man to arrive on the mainland from the Solomons since American occupation, is pictured in San Fran yesterday. He told how Australian flyers carried empty bottles with them, which they tossed out of their planes following the bombing of Tulagi. The bottles "whistled all the way down," scaring the natives and the Japanese invaders, Huff said at press conference.

Bottles flung as a prank. Not a word about his fellow U.S. Navy men on *Vincennes*, *Quincy*, and *Astoria*. The photo was accompanied by this disturbing headline:

MARINES FIGHT OFF NEW JAP LANDING

No, the Marines were far from mopping up. Meanwhile, help was on the way. A photo inside the September 6 edition showed Clark Gable, having enlisted in the U.S. Army Air Force, and now in officer candidate school at Miami Beach, getting his rifle inspected.

On September 11, the sinking or damaging of three Japanese destroyers by U.S. Navy planes in the Solomons area was reported. Two days later, a headline over another story claimed:

U.S. UNITS BAG 96 JAP PLANES AT SOLOMONS

Below it, another headline, "Battleship, cruiser hit in record air victory." Although the details were a bit off, both of these delayed reports were apparently from the Battle of the Eastern Solomons, which had indeed cost the Japanese a large number of aircraft, a light carrier, and a destroyer.

Each day's news revealed additional success and more reason for the folks back home to scour vacant lots for the scrap metal drive, another frequent front-page concern. But the news was often delivered with admonitions. A story headlined "Report on Nazi Convoy Battle" tells of word coming from the Atlantic of German submarines converging on Allied ships, with a small box inserted within the story:

"Warning—this news comes from an enemy source. Bear in mind there is likelihood it was designed for propaganda purposes."

Inside the section, the publisher of the *Democrat and Chronicle*, Frank Gannett, was one of the featured speakers at a forum called "News, Censorship and Morale." Gannett was quoted extensively, including his comment, "The American people have shown that they can stand bad news. The disaster at Pearl Harbor, the beating that Gen. Stillwell admitted he took in Burma and the loss of the Philippines did not destroy our morale."

The September 6 headline "Allies Admit U-Pac Attack" confirmed the bad news that had been reported by the "enemy source" a few days earlier. Although, it hedged, the claims that nineteen ships were sunk are "nowhere near the truth and bloated to the bursting point."

The next day, this big headline:

CARRIER YORKTOWN SUNK AT MIDWAY, NAVY REVEALS

This was September 17. *Yorktown* had been lost on June 7.

The next day, somewhere between the harrowing headline proclaiming Stalingrad's fate hanging in the balance and an advertisement cautioning, "Look out for wartime constipation," came another delayed report:

> The 1,500-ton destroyer *Jarvis*, with possibly 172 men aboard, has vanished in the southwest Pacific and is assumed to have been sunk by Japanese submarines or aircraft, the Navy announced yesterday, and the speedy auxiliary transport *Little* also has been lost.

Their destruction raised announced U.S. naval losses in that conflict to five ships sunk and five damaged, as against at least 22 Japanese vessels sunk or damaged.

Previously it had been revealed the destroyer *Blue*, the auxiliary transport *Calhoun* and an unidentified cruiser had been sunk in the Solomons and two cruisers, two destroyers and one transport damaged.

Jarvis's newspaper obituary appeared five weeks after it actually had sunk. Heavily damaged while protecting the transports during the Guadalcanal landings, the destroyer had limped away for repairs, narrowly missing the Japanese fleet as it arrived at Savo Island. With its radios disabled, *Jarvis* was unable to transmit a warning and continued on. But thinking it was a cruiser that had escaped the slaughter in the early morning hours of August 9, the Japanese sent thirty-one airplanes after the ship and sank it with the loss of its entire crew of 233 men.

According to that news report's scorecard, U.S. Navy losses to that point in the war were forty-three ships sunk or scuttled, twelve damaged. Japanese ship losses were estimated at four hundred lost or damaged.

On September 29, readers learned, "Smashing with terrific force at the Japanese in both the Solomon and Aleutian islands, Army-Navy-Marine corps airmen in the last five days have destroyed at least 49 enemy planes and damaged five ships, one of which probably sank, without the loss of a single American plane in combat."

Just a few pages from this triumphant report was more discussion about the suppression of wartime news. Byron Price, the government's director of censorship, told yet another gathering of publishers that although their newspapers had done well in not publishing information that might be of value to the enemy, they "have done a poor job of informing the people why some of the information has to be withheld."

If newspapers weren't publishing information that would be of value to the enemy, they were also publishing fiction that was of little value to the people. Often the information that the American public received arrived piecemeal and out of context.

"U.S. Reveals Japs Sank Two Transports," the *Democrat and Chronicle* told its readers on October 1, the news still trailing real time in the Solomons.

"Small Losses in Pacific Attacks Reported."

These were *George F. Elliott*, an elderly passenger liner converted into a troop ship, which had been set afire when a Japanese torpedo plane

crashed into it during the same battle in which *Jarvis* was initially damaged, and *Gregory*, a World War I destroyer converted into a transport.
Gregory had been lost on the morning of September 5 near Savo Island,
in the same battle with three Japanese destroyers that claimed the navy
transport *Little*. Despite the picture that was being presented to readers of
a Solomon Islands campaign in which the Japanese forces were being
"wiped out," the Japanese were actually very much still in the battle.

And then, the slap of a rolled-up newspaper landing on the front porch
on the morning of October 13 announced to Rochester and the world
what had happened to Ernie and his shipmates:

3 BIG CRUISERS LOST, NAVY REVEALS

After more than two months of drifting first in the water off Savo
Island and then through the bureaucracy of the Office of Censorship, the
newspaper reports were startlingly frank.

"Heavy Loss of Life Reported from Naval Action," read one headline.

"Survivor Reveals Sharks Periled Wounded Men," another reported
breathlessly.

A sailor from *Astoria*, a Texan named Lynn Hager, was interviewed.

"We'd been fighting constantly since the beginning of the Tulagi battle, thirty-six hours before," he said.

"We expected a Jap naval force the next morning and we needed rest."

It is Hager who reveals in the story that ships were machine-gunning
sharks in an attempt to keep them off the survivors struggling in the
water.

But it was not long before the home front had reason to celebrate once
again. On the very next morning, the *Democrat and Chronicle* greeted its
readers with:

U.S. FLEET SINKS SIX JAP WARSHIPS

"Thus did Uncle Sam's Bluejackets and aircraft avenge the loss of the
cruisers *Quincy*, *Vincennes* and *Astoria*, which were sunk August 9 during the initial phase of the American offensive against the Solomons," the
Associated Press reported. "Thirty minutes after the first gun was fired,
the battered Jap force was in retreat."

Some wartime license was in effect here. This was what was later to
be called the Battle of Cape Esperance, the third of the naval battles
surrounding the Guadalcanal campaign. It was indeed a U.S. victory,

although the Japanese losses were one cruiser and three destroyers sunk and a second cruiser heavily damaged. American losses were one destroyer sunk, one cruiser and one destroyer heavily damaged.

And although two of the Japanese ships were sunk by marauding American aircraft after the action had broken off, one aspect of the news report was dead on. As had been the case in the loss of the four Allied cruisers two months earlier, the Battle of Cape Esperance lasted only thirty minutes. It was an echo, once again, of the delayed dispatch filed from the doomed U.S. squadron "bound for 'somewhere,'" and its training exercise. "It was all over in what seemed like a few minutes."

All it took was a few minutes. The best of naval design had been easily eclipsed by the technology to destroy these ships.

TWENTY-FOUR

The Erie Canal is history that wound through the geography of Ernie's early years. He conquered it on his epic canoe trip in 1931, swam in it during the summers, and learned how to dive off the gates of Pittsford's Lock 32 on the New York State Barge Canal, as it had been known since 1918, which gave boats a twenty-five-foot boost to the next level on the way to Buffalo. "I was fourteen, fifteen years old at the time, and I remember watching a girl diving from the top of it," Ernie declares.

"I said, 'Well, if a girl can do it, I can do it.'"

He could. Ernie was developing into a strong swimmer. He remembers summers at his parents' vacation home in Crystal Beach on Canandaigua Lake, when he'd slip into the water and swim to the far shore, "a good two miles away," he says. "I was a stupid kid. I'd catch hell from my parents for that."

But then he'd go and do it again.

The winter of 1933 to 1934, when Ernie was seventeen, more adventure came calling again from the direction of the canal. "The only time in my lifetime they didn't drain it," he says. The three musketeers couldn't let this opportunity slide by. They plotted out a skating trip starting from Lock 32. Destination: Newark, nearly twenty-nine miles away.

"I skated a little farther along than the other two guys," Ernie says. "I always try to be first in everything, I guess." The ice on the canal was about four inches thick, good enough to keep everyone moving along. Except where someone had cut a large fishing hole. Ice had just started to form over the spot when Ernie slid to a stop right over it, looking back to check on the progress of his companions. Then he disappeared from sight.

"I'm in the water; it's like the lights are turned off," he says. "I'm looking up. 'Where is that hole?' I saw something that looked like a twenty-five-watt bulb. 'That must be it.'"

Ernie pushed himself up from the bottom, twelve feet below the ice. He swam toward the light, and it grew larger and larger until he emerged from the water. "By that time, the guys were there to help me out," he says.

They gathered brush and built a fire on the shore.

"Fortunately, one of the guys smoked, so we had matches," Ernie says.

"They kept changing clothes with me. But basically, I stood and froze while my clothes were drying."

And then the boys continued the trip. "We were only four miles into it," Ernie says with a shrug. They skated to Newark and then back.

He could have died in that water.

"One of my nine lives," Ernie would joke.

Perhaps another life was terminated after falling down the basement stairs at his Madison Terrace home. Ernie's first wife, Ruth, died in a fall down the stairs at her home. Or maybe colon cancer could have gotten him. It is the third-most common cancer afflicting Americans.

* * *

Ernie thought he could talk about his war experience. But the nightmares were just below the surface. He talked about his divorce, the death of two of his wives. He talked with unnerving frankness, humor even, about the series of surgeries that he'd endured over the past decade. He talked about joining the navy, the training, the days leading up to his departure from Pearl Harbor, and the twenty-two months he spent afterward on Maui. But when it came to the Battle of Savo Island, he backed off. The nightmares returned. The screams of his fellow sailors in the water were too loud.

Aging veterans speak of similar experiences every evening on the History Channel. They have described these events to writers. Some of the vets break down in tears, even after all these years. Others choose simply to not talk about what they witnessed, except in the most veiled ways. That's Ernie. His family knew he was a World War II navy man, but it wasn't until the final years of his life that they knew that he was on a ship that sunk in battle. For the most part, they had never heard of *Vincennes*.

I have said this much already: A muggy and extraordinarily dark evening smothered the southwestern Pacific Solomon Islands on August 9, 1942. No moon illuminated the waters around Guadalcanal Island and its accompanying string of islands, including Florida and Tulagi, with its golf course and cricket club built by the British as a way of dragging Western civilization to this part of the world. And, just to the north of Guadalcanal, Savo Island.

But much of what we know—and thought we knew—of what naval historian Samuel Eliot Morison describes in *The Two-Ocean War* as "probably the worst defeat ever inflicted on the United States Navy in a fair fight" remained a secret from the American public for months afterward. Some facts were obscured for decades. Misconceptions and deceptions remain to this day.

As *Vincennes* charted a course that would end abruptly off Savo Island, the attitude of the day—often a mocking dismissal of the Imperial Japanese Navy and its ships—did little to prepare the Allies for the battles ahead. In *Fighting Fleets*, an overview of the world's navies of the day, author Critchell Rimington writes, "Japanese cruisers are known to be compact and highly efficient fighting machines, even though their uneven decks and pagoda-like conning towers have been the cause of much naval amusement." This was a book published in 1943, with the outcome of the Pacific War very much in doubt. Near the back of *Fighting Fleets*, in an addenda labeled "Naval War Losses," is a list of warship losses by nation in World War II until that point.

These ships of the Imperial Japanese Navy, "the cause of much naval amusement," had already done their dark work. Turning to the final pages of *Fighting Fleets*, we see that *Vincennes*, *Astoria*, and *Quincy* had taken their places under the heading for U.S. losses.

This arrogance extended into the highest ranks of Allied command. In their 1992 book *Disaster in the Pacific: New Light on the Battle of Savo Island*, writers Denis and Peggy Warner, with Sadao Seno, point out that the commander of land-based air forces in the southwest Pacific, Lieutenant General George C. Kenney, embraced racist clichés and dangerously underestimated his Japanese opponents.

"Too much of their population," Kenney said, "is peasant class—rice planters, fishermen, rickshaw pullers—who are too dumb, too slow-moving and utterly lacking in mechanical knowledge and adaptability."

And this was in September 1944, after *Vincennes*, *Astoria*, and *Quincy* had been joined on the *Fighting Fleets* addenda by many, many more U.S. ships.

Disaster in the Pacific reveals more errors in Allied judgment as the two fleets closed for battle.

"Neither the *Vincennes* nor the *Quincy*, which had only recently arrived from the Atlantic, had held night battle exercises or night target practice for at least 15 months," the Warners write. Most of the Allied commanders believed that a night action between warships was unlikely. Yet, the Warners point out, "hard training and night fighting were the twin pillars of naval preparation" for the Japanese navy—and had been since 1904, when Japanese destroyers surprised the Russian navy at Port Arthur, initiating the Russo-Japanese War. Since then, the Warners write, surprise "had been the key element in Japanese military thinking."

American preparations for the coming Guadalcanal invasion had not gone well, despite assembling a vast task force of U.S. and Australian ships. The war correspondent reporting back by delayed dispatch to the readers of the *Democrat and Chronicle* had adoringly described the "impressive preview of things to come today in a slashing, thunderous drill with live ammunition which was marked by the fine timing of a crack football team."

But in reality, the Fiji Islands dress rehearsal for the retaking of Guadalcanal and Tulagi was a failure. The landing craft couldn't get ashore because of dangerous reefs, and the exercise was reduced to the cruisers lobbing their eight-inch, 335-pound shells at the island while airplanes practiced strafing runs on beach crabs.

Yet the landings on Guadalcanal and Tulagi on August 7 went as smoothly as anyone in the Allied command dared hope. The ships had closed in on the islands at night under cloud cover. *Vincennes* was among the big ships firing at hoped-for Japanese targets in the darkness, the shells red arcs in the night sky. As dawn arrived, the marines' landing on Guadalcanal was startlingly unopposed, the Japanese having withdrawn into the jungle. It was a tough fight on Tulagi before the Americans gained control.

And then, the combatants for the Battle of Savo Island assembled for their fight.

The U.S. and Japanese navies entered the war with eighteen cruisers apiece, offspring of the 1922 Washington Naval Treaty. With Europe in ruins after World War I, the thinking was that the next war won't be so bad if there are fewer and smaller guns. The treaty limited cruisers to ten thousand tons displacement and no armaments larger than eight-inch guns. Japanese cruisers built in the 1930s tended to creep over ten thousand tons, in violation of the treaty, but most analysts rate the fleets evenly. The major difference in the two navies' cruisers was in torpedo tubes. The U.S. cruisers went without, whereas the Japanese cruisers were armed with torpedoes that far outperformed any other navy's version of the weapon.

Yet the ships that carried Ernie and his crewmates into battle were rapidly becoming anachronistic, anyway. The naval thinkers were now concluding that surface gun battles between large ships were in their twilight. In fact, four American cruisers launched just before the attack on Pearl Harbor; the Atlanta class represented an abrupt change in U.S. naval strategy. These ships were armed with torpedo tubes, as though the cruisers were expected to engage in the same close-range exchanges with an enemy as destroyers had done.

These new ships had depth charges as well, replicating a destroyer's antisubmarine duties. But most importantly, the main turrets were now fixed with smaller five-inch cannon, along with a host of smaller guns, all faster firing weapons more suitable for antiaircraft defense than the eight-inch cannon of the last decade's heavy cruisers. The Atlanta class also eliminated the scout planes that cruisers typically carried, planes that would play a key role in the Battle of Savo Island, even though they never left their ships. Cruiser-based scout aircraft would be superfluous in the radar-enhanced navies of the future. With the increasing emphasis on the construction of aircraft carriers, plenty of planes would be at hand. Navy thinkers were anticipating the cruiser's role evolving into carrier escorts invited to the vast Pacific dance.

Neither the commanders of the U.S. fleet patrolling off Savo Island nor the equipment they had on hand had caught up to the strategies emerging from the drafting boards. Indeed, two days after the landings on Guadalcanal and Tulagi, the navy pulled from the battle its three aircraft carriers, fearful of losing them. Naval battles in the first six months of the war had cost it two carriers, *Lexington* and *Yorktown*. So the air was under the control of whatever aircraft were based on the bomb-cratered airstrip that the marines had captured at Guadalcanal and what the Japanese could bring with them to the fight. Since they had just lost four aircraft carriers at the Battle of Midway, it wouldn't be enough to affect the battle.

Curiously missing from this fight was Task Force 1, the American Pacific fleet of battleships that included three pulled from the shallow mud bottom of Pearl Harbor that had been thoroughly modernized in the eight months since the attack: *Maryland*, *Pennsylvania*, and *Tennessee*. But with German U-boats terrorizing the convoys of the Atlantic, oil transports were being diverted from the Pacific. Moving fuel around the Pacific was a logistical nightmare. And the seven battleships of Task Force 1 were the navy equivalents of the 1957 Cadillac Eldorado Brougham: gas hogs.

Also curiously missing from the Battle of Savo Island was the commander of the landing force cruiser screen, Rear Admiral Victor Crutchley, another anachronism, a British Royal Navy veteran of the World War I Battle of Jutland. On August 8, hours before the battle that night and early the next morning, he took the cruiser *Australia* out of the southern group of patrolling cruisers so that he could meet with the commander of the Guadalcanal landings without telling his ship captains what he was up to or who was in charge.

All of this worked against the Allied fleet as Japanese Vice Admiral Gunichi Mikawa's seven cruisers and one destroyer, each flying a twenty-three-foot-long white pennant so that they could more easily identify their comrades in the battle, rushed under cover of darkness from the north through New Georgia Sound, "the Slot," as it was called by the Allies.

Each card played seemed to fall the way of the Japanese, whose ships were hidden on the edge of a storm squall, lightning occasionally flickering through the dark clouds, as they fortuitously passed unseen between two U.S. destroyers to reach the rest of the Allied fleet. Blunder after blunder was committed by the doomed Allies, who had split their forces, misread their radars, dismissed Japanese scout planes and ships as their own, erred on the positions of their own ships, and, as Japanese shells first began hitting the Australian cruiser *Canberra* at 1:43 a.m., mistook the explosions as the actions of the marines fighting the Japanese on the islands.

From the opening seconds, the battle was illuminated by flares dropped from Japanese floatplanes, star shells fired by the U.S. cruiser *Chicago*, and then flames from *Canberra*, which was out of the fight just two minutes after it had begun, struck by as many as thirty shells before it could train its guns on the enemy. Then *Chicago*, after a brief exchange with the Japanese squadron, inexplicably charged off in the wrong direction and out of the battle.

Just as the U.S. Navy had been taken by surprise at Pearl Harbor and as the Japanese had been taken by surprise by the Allied landings in the Solomons two days earlier, now the Allies had been taken by surprise by the Imperial Japanese Navy. Having scattered the southern group of Allied ships in mere minutes, the Japanese circled south of Savo Island, a small volcanic peak jutting up in the middle of the Slot. They were heading east and then north toward the northern group seven miles away led by *Vincennes*, which was unaware of—as James D. Hornfischer writes in his 2011 book, *Neptune's Inferno: The U.S. Navy at Guadalcanal*—"the spectacular catastrophe of the preceding four hundred seconds."

Mikawa was astonishingly gracious when he wrote afterward about what took place:

> The element of surprise worked to our advantage and enabled us to destroy every target taken under fire. I was greatly impressed, however, by the courageous action of the northern group of U.S. cruisers. They fought heroically despite heavy damage sustained before they were ready for battle. Had they had even a few minutes' warning of our approach, the results of the action would have been different.

In fact, the Allies had been warned. An Australian Lockheed Hudson bomber spotted the Japanese fleet the afternoon before the battle. Morison's history of this moment carries the day; he wrote that the plane had not broken radio silence but merely had returned to its base and—the story taking on outlandish embellishments with time—the crew dawdled over tea before reporting their sighting.

Disaster in the Pacific, using testimony from the day and a report that wasn't declassified until 1973, exonerates that air crew. Who knows why—perhaps the search for a scapegoat—but for decades the navy and

Morison's version prevailed. We now know otherwise. The Allied high command was aware that the Japanese were within striking distance. Commanders and captains were notified. But proper preparations were not made.

And the obvious was ignored even as flames from the first of the Allied ships lit the night sky: "WARNING—WARNING—STRANGE SHIPS ENTERING HARBOR," the U.S. destroyer *Patterson* radioed. The message never reached the bridge of *Vincennes*, leading the northern group. Instead, a message on yet another course change was delivered. The message did reach *Astoria*, but no one thought to relay it to gunnery, in preparation for battle. *Quincy* never heard the warning at all.

Inexplicably, uncertainty followed what should have been a very clear next message: *Astoria*, *Quincy*, and *Vincennes* were suddenly illuminated by spotlights from the Japanese ships at 7,500, 9,500, and 10,500 yards, respectively, in misting rain and light breezes. *Vincennes* Captain Frederick Riefkohl ordered a radio message be sent to whatever fellow ship that was to turn off the lights. An eruption of water just in front of Riefkohl's ship moments later, at 1:55 a.m., announced the arrival of Japanese shells. The Americans could even see them, black shapes with an orange glow in the night sky.

Confusion reigned—were those our ships?—even as the shells began striking *Vincennes*, first hitting the carpenter shop, the bridge, the hangar, and the communications antennae. The hangar was particularly problematic. Although the fuel had been drained from the five aircraft carried by *Astoria* and *Vincennes*, the SOC Seagull floatplanes on all three ships nevertheless went up in flames, providing the Japanese gunners with carnival-like shooting gallery targets, while also allowing the Japanese to turn off their own searchlights and fire from the protection of darkness.

Minutes into the battle, Riefkohl still seemed to believe that his ship might be the victim of friendly fire, sending blinker signals and hoisting signal flags. The captain of *Astoria* thought this might be the case as well. Still the shells and torpedoes came, as the Japanese ships separated into two lines with the three American cruisers in the middle, delivering death from both sides.

Official battle damage reports can be a breathtaking mix of analytical and brutal reading, the conclusions as clinical as an autopsy. In the case of *Vincennes*, *Quincy*, and *Astoria*, the autopsy was issued on September 3, 1943, more than a year after the battle. I found it on the internet. An actual copy of tight, single-spaced lines hammered out on manual type-writers by clerks sitting in the Navy Department Bureau of Ships in Washington, D.C., thousands of miles from the battle.

The shell hits sustained by the ships are frequently numbered in the report. Of *Vincennes*, the investigators write, "The carpenter shop just aft of the hangar was hit three or four times (Hits Nos. 52, 53, and 54) and fires were started in this compartment."

The destruction reached deep into the ship, to the boiler rooms:

> The No. 1 fireroom is believed to have been hit by either a projectile or torpedo as there were no surviving personnel from this space. . . . The intensely hot fragments from a High Explosive projectile inside a ship have few if any equals in setting fires within confined spaces. . . . Topside personnel accounted for the majority of the casualties. . . . At least 57 hits were received in the spaces discussed above. Undoubtedly, as in *Quincy*, there were many other hits in these and surrounding spaces which were not reported.

There were far too many holes to be plugged by mattresses backed with two-by-fours. The Japanese could hardly believe their good fortune, as "every salvo caused another enemy ship to burst into flames," one Japanese veteran of the battle later wrote.

> For incredible minutes the turrets of enemy ships remained in their trained-in, secured positions, and we stood amazed. Yet thankful while they did not bear on us. Strings of machine-gun tracers wafted back and forth between the enemy and ourselves, but such minor counter-efforts merely made a colorful spectacle, and gave us no concern.

One dramatic photo taken from a Japanese cruiser shows *Quincy* illuminated by Japanese spotlights and enveloped in brightly lit, billowing smoke. Off to starboard is a ball of flame searing the night sky. That's *Vincennes*.

The official battle report continues: "In all three ships these fires were fed by topside paint, life jackets, signal flags, airplanes, airplane spare tails, wings, parachutes, ships' boats, lubricating oil and kerosene, which made the area between the bridge and the after bulkhead of the hangar an inferno beyond human endurance."

Aboard *Vincennes*, this area included the carpenter shop—Ernie's station—and its stores of highly flammable materials. Flames licked up the paint with which Ernie and his mates in the carpenter shop had covered the ship as it churned across the Pacific. More hits knocked out the range finders, gun-control electronics, the secondary five-inch guns, and inter-ship radio, and firefighting became impossible with the water mains brok-en. Steering control from the bridge was lost. The damage report tells of an eight-inch shell—hit No. 7—penetrating the second turret but not exploding, instead setting fire to exposed powder. These fighting ships, designed to deal damage to their enemies, were proving deadly to their own crews.

"Attention is invited to paragraphs 25 and 45," write the authors of the official battle report, "in which the 5-inch/25-caliber ready-service am-munition exploded as a result of projectile hits. . . . When so ignited, cartridge cases may be expected to jump out by rocket action in a flaming condition, and to burn on deck or to roast other charges so that they too ignite in succession."

Vincennes, its guns manned by incinerated corpses, was doomed. Two torpedoes from the Japanese cruiser *Chokai* may have struck it in the port side, although the reports are never in total agreement, so furious was the assault. Flaming wreckage and live shells were dumped overboard, and the gun turrets were now running on auxiliary diesel generators or were being cranked by hand. The ship was a tangle of smoke, steam, and dead sailors. The decks were slippery with blood.

Belowdecks, breathable air was becoming difficult to find. Yet *Vin-cennes* still managed to hit the Japanese cruiser *Kinugasa* with a round of eight-inch shells. But in the twenty two–minute fight, it managed only two full salvos from its nine eight-inch guns and another two six-gun salvoes.

"What a scene!" wrote *Life* magazine photographer Ralph Morse. He had been taking pictures of the combat on Guadalcanal and had locked his precious negatives in a safe aboard *Vincennes* when he learned it would be heading stateside for overhaul after this action. He lost every-thing except his life.

"The sky was lit up with shelling and fires on ships," Morse wrote. "Ships were shelling ships and ships were sinking all around us. I kept shooting like mad. Sailors were being hit all around us, and sailors were being killed just next to me."

What a scene, indeed. As Hornfischer writes so pointedly in *Neptune's Inferno*, "It was about 2:40 in the morning when Admiral Crutchley, from the bridge of the *Australia*, observed a trio of objects burning on the sea between Savo and Florida islands and wondered what calamity he had missed."

Word from Captain Riefkohl was passed around to abandon ship shortly after an apparent third torpedo hit by the light cruiser *Yubari* set *Vincennes* on a shuddering, lurching list to port. The wounded were helped into life jackets. Life rafts that hadn't been burned were heaved into the water, and lines were draped over the side of the ship for men to climb down into the sea while others held flashlights. Some men simply jumped into the water. *Vincennes* continued to heel to port, its entire superstructure aflame and beginning to crumple. It was probably the first and only time that any man on board had witnessed the astonishing sight of steel burning. *Vincennes*'s propellers emerged from the water, a sword of Damocles waving over the men already in the sea who were struggling to cling to floating debris. The ship slipped lower into the water and began to capsize; now its crew, including Riefkohl, could simply step into the Georgia Sound. *Vincennes* continued to roll until its mast smacked the water, almost hitting Riefkohl, its decks a flaming mass of scout planes and broken teakwood, the smokestacks dipping into the water until the ship turned turtle and went down by the bow.

Just as that war correspondent wrote of the Allied dress rehearsal at the Fiji Islands, "It was over in what seemed like a few minutes."

Twenty-two, in fact. At 2:15 a.m., the Japanese ships ceased firing and withdrew back up the sound. *Quincy* and *Vincennes* went down within fifteen minutes of each other, *Quincy* first around 2:35 a.m. Both ships filled the warm, shark-infested sea with more than one thousand oil-covered sailors, many wounded or in shock, clinging to mattresses and shell casings and rafts and furniture and lumber, worried as well that in the dark confusion they might get run over by a ship. The sailors drifted for six and seven hours, in some cases longer, before the destroyers *Ellet* and *Wilson* came to the rescue of most of *Quincy*'s men.

The bulk of the crew of *Vincennes*, which sank more than a mile from *Quincy*, was scooped up by the destroyers *Mugford* and *Helm*. Morse, the *Life* photographer, was in the water for eight hours.

"Luckily, it was a very noisy battle with shells going off and torpedoes hitting ships," he wrote. "I guess any shark in his right mind got the hell out of there."

Large and small acts of heroism continued through the night. Men on the surviving ships dove into the water to rescue the shipwrecked. *Astoria* and *Canberra* survived into the next day before sinking, *Canberra* scuttled by American torpedoes.

In the few, furious minutes that were the Battle of Savo Island, the Japanese had fired 1,844 shells of various caliber, reporting 159 definite hits and another 64 probables. And the hits were effective, the shells timed to explode not on contact, but after penetrating deep inside the target. Of the nine eight-inch gun turrets on the three American cruisers, six were destroyed by direct hits. The American ships got off 471 shots, recording ten hits. Allied losses on the four sunken cruisers, the damaged ships, and on the destroyer *Jarvis*, when it was set upon and sunk afterward, were 1,275 men killed, more than 700 wounded. Japanese losses were about fifty men killed, perhaps twice that many wounded.

The area became known as Iron Bottom Sound for the number of warships that came to rest on the seabed. *Vincennes*, *Quincy*, *Astoria*, and *Canberra* were merely the first. By the end of the battles, each side had contributed 24 large ships to the graveyard and lost nearly the same number of aircraft each, 450. As many as five thousand American sailors died and four thousand Japanese during the Guadalcanal campaign, which labored on until the Japanese finally withdrew in February 1943. As for the U.S. Marines and Army troops who stormed ashore, the official death count is 1,592. For the Japanese defenders, about 20,800 dead.

* * *

Those are the numbers. Here's another number: five hundred fathoms. That is the approximate depth at which Robert Ballard found two of the lost cruisers from the Battle of Savo Island more than a half-century later.

Ballard is the celebrity oceanographer best known for leading the expedition that discovered the ruins of *Titanic* on the floor of the Atlantic Ocean in 1985, at the tail end of an expedition secretly financed by the U.S. Navy to find two submarines it had lost in the 1960s, *Thresher* and *Scorpion*. He has since used submersibles and remote-controlled vehicles to explore other wrecks as well, all with their own violent histories: the German battleship *Bismarck* in 1989, the torpedoed ocean liner *Lusitania* in 1993, *Yorktown* in 1998, even President John F. Kennedy's PT-109 in 2002 (they found a torpedo tube). Film crews accompanied Ballard, converting this gruesome archaeology into entertainment delivered directly to viewers in their living rooms.

And this may be acceptable, so long as we learn the lessons of history.

The lessons of history? Ballard spent three weeks at Iron Bottom Sound in 1992 after a mostly unsuccessful 1991 expedition, and this time quickly uncovered *Canberra*, then *Quincy*. His expedition discovered thirteen wrecks in all from the Guadalcanal campaign's naval actions, although *Vincennes* was not one of them. The resulting documentary and lavishly illustrated book detailing the finds, *Robert Ballard's Guadalcanal*, show the Japanese battleship *Kirishima* lying upside down, its guns and command centers smashed into the mud, a huge anchor chain wrapped around one propeller like a leash entangling a dog. Of *Canberra*, we see a starboard anchor still attached to the hull and a forward turret with its eight-inch guns. Of *Quincy*, the bridge, looking remarkably intact despite having taken a hit that killed nearly everyone there, including the ship's captain. The ships are covered in marine growth and are generally so battered that American, Japanese, and Australian wreckage lose all nationality. The green patina of the photos reveals the destroyer *Monssen*'s torpedo tubes and a hole in the hull of the Japanese destroyer *Ayanami* where a wheel that was used to aim the torpedoes can be seen. And unidentifiable broken steel, remnants from a ship that had only recently been designed as the future of naval warfare, *Atlanta*. It was destroyed during the night battle of November 12 and 13 off Guadalcanal, its useless state-of-the-art design sunk not only by Japanese shells and torpedoes, but by U.S. shells accidentally fired at it in the confusion. And there is one hundred feet of the destroyer *Barton*'s bow, the section where the ship broke in half lost in the darkness.

The darkness. In truth, without intense lights illuminating only short spans of this mess, a diver never would know that most of this was sitting on the mud floor of Iron Bottom Sound, the steel slowly and quietly giving way to the saltwater. Photographs present only quick shards of the damage suffered by these ships, not only during the battle, but during their difficult freefalls to the ocean floor. So as is frequently the case with Ballard's expeditions, the renowned marine painter Ken Marschall was brought in to give viewers the full picture of what these war relics look like today.

Canberra's big guns, never used in this battle, point crazily, as do *Quincy*'s. The water rushing past the muzzles as the ships sank created this nonsensical arrangement. At *Quincy*'s two forward turrets, the guns aim upward, as though this game fighter had been firing at its enemies even as it dropped out of sight. Its bow is ripped off and completely missing just before the first turret, the stern and aft deck collapsed and bent upward.

In the deep, eerie blue light that Marschall gave each scene, the ships look like toys at the bottom of an aquarium.

It is an elegant, ugly futility. In the final pages of *The Winds of War*, Navy Commander Pug Henry stands on an overlook in the early morning darkness, looking down on the wrecked battleships after the attack on Pearl Harbor.

"He could almost picture God the Father looking down with sad wonder at this mischief," Herman Wouk writes. "In a world so rich and lovely, could his children find nothing better to do than to dig iron from the ground and work it into vast grotesque engines for blowing each other up?"

History predicts that will never be the case for mankind in general. But sailing Lake Ontario for all these decades, Ernie Coleman had done so. He found something better to do.

TWENTY-FIVE

Over the years Charlie Ross came to suspect that important pieces were missing from Ernie's story.

"He never talked about the war at all," Charlie says. "It was 2008 before I ever got anything out of him. All he ever told us is he was stationed in Hawaii. He was up at our house for Thanksgiving, and I just asked him, 'What else did you do in the war? You must have done something else.'"

Ernie's response was prescient: "What, are you writing a book?"

"I just told him, 'Well, you're getting up there. . . .'" But now Charlie knew, after all of these years, that Ernie's war experience had been more than Hawaii. A few months earlier he had asked Ernie if he'd been on a ship. Yes, *Vincennes*, Ernie had said, offering nothing else.

Charlie looked it up. He read about Savo Island. Now, on this Thanksgiving, Charlie pressed Ernie on the matter.

"He said, 'I have nightmares when I talk about it.'"

All of that time had passed and still *Vincennes* haunted him. Yet the nightmares hadn't chased Ernie from the water. That final night on *Vincennes* was for the most part something that Ernie, Charlie says, "had put somewhere else."

A distant compartment where it wouldn't be heard from as he moved on with his life. Returning from the war, Ernie had continued to sail and win races, undeterred by the vastness of a lake that stretches across the horizon in much the same manner as the South Pacific, paying no mind to low-lying clouds or distant shores that can look like warships, if you allow your mind to take you there. Or the rumble of thunder from an approaching storm, so much like gunfire.

* * *

Everyone on both sides of the docks, the Genesee Yacht Club and the Rochester Yacht Club, was familiar with both sides of Ernie. The modest old carpenter and the aging, fiercely competitive lake racer.

"See that gray shed over there?" State Supreme Court Justice Kenny Fisher says one morning. He's standing at the front door of the RYC and pointing across the parking lot and docks, now empty for the winter season.

"Ernie's there almost every morning, with all the old hands. They get together for coffee."

"He is a landmark in Rochester," Roger Libby says. "Even at the Sodus Bay Yacht Club, the Canandaigua Yacht Club, they know him. You tell them you sailed with Ernie, that opens up a whole twenty minutes of stories."

Roger's got them. He and his wife, Diane, are Maine natives. They came to Rochester in the 1970s, twentysomethings recruited as chemical engineers by Eastman Kodak at a time when the photography giant was the heart and business soul of the city. It was after a chance meeting when their boats were sharing dock space that Ernie recruited the Libbys to crew with him on *Desire*. It was a relationship that lasted nearly twenty years, the Libbys sailing with Ernie well into the '90s.

"We kind of hit it off," Roger says. "He really became my Rochester father. My father died in '83, and we were like Ernie's kids. We got along like family. We argued like family. When Diane started racing, Evie would even come out. She'd be on *Desire* on Tuesdays, which were not quite as competitive races."

But make no mistake, Roger says. Ernie made it clear why they were out there.

"For ten, twelve years, for small boats under thirty feet, we were the team to beat," he says.

"We put more trophies in those two yacht clubs than any other boat. We raced hard; we raced to win. When the race was over, the race was over. We went into the club and had a good time. We didn't debate it."

The Libbys retired to Mars Hill, Maine, in the early part of the new century, as Kodak was tumbling from the city map in a dizzying economic slide of downsizing and planned implosions of deserted buildings.

Roger doesn't remember the races with the exacting precision that Ernie showed off, but the feel of those races hasn't left him.

"The ones that really stand out were the Scotch Bonnet light races," Roger says. The ones across the lake to Canada, looping around tiny Scotch Bonnet Island, and then a return to Rochester.

"And the ones that were scary, with treacherous thunderstorms and lightning, when the storms were so close you could hear the rigging singing."

The key, Roger adds, was consistency. And crew members knowing their precise roles.

"We would get into tacking duels with another boat owned by—oh, what was his name?—Denny Doyle, on *Bangalore*. He had just one large mainsail, so for him to tack was very easy. He would trail right behind us, hoping we'd make a mistake and then he would shoot by us. But we rarely made mistakes.

"I knew the basics of sailing when we first met. Ernie is probably the person who taught me 90 percent of what I know about sailing. He stayed up with technology changes, installing compasses and telltales, then he got LORAN. I used most of the electronics, while he sailed by the seat of his pants, because he was that good. Sometimes things like GPS, on long-distance racing it could be difficult to get Ernie to believe the instruments. You'd tell him we were starting to drift and the winds were changing, but he tended to go with his instincts. He slowly came around to modern technology. It helped us, and his ability to helm the boat and feel it, and my wife's ability to trim the sails.

"I wouldn't trade our relationship for anything in the world. We worked and learned together. He was a family man, down to earth. He'd give you the shirt off his back."

Ernie shared his vast life experience with the Libbys.

Except, Roger says, "he never talked about the war."

Craig Roth sailed with Ernie on Wednesdays for a decade. A decade during which the suddenly scuffed-up Ernie was a construction of bailing wire and spit as he piloted *Desire*.

"He holds up great," Craig says. While he's on the phone discussing Ernie, Craig's parrot can be heard in the background, whistling in agreement.

"I'll be amazed when I'm his age if I can do that."

Craig doesn't mean whistling; he means sailing. The stories Ernie told were more than a bonus. With *Desire* not quite the competitive boat that it once was, shooting the breeze as the sails filled with air was now the point.

"I just enjoy being around him," Craig says. "He's had a lot of experiences; he has a lot of stories. He talks about when he sailed smaller boats. The Sunfish and I think it was the Snipe. His history in the navy during World War II."

Retired from the Department of Social Services's Fair Hearing Unit, Craig was never in the navy himself, but his father was, and Craig was born a navy brat. Perhaps that association brought the service stories out of Ernie.

"He talks about his time in Hawaii," Craig says.

"He was a carpenter's mate. He talks about the different ships he was on. The *Saratoga*. But he wasn't on that one long. It took a torpedo and came back to port, and they took Ernie off before it left again."

Saratoga? That's a bit of Ernie's war history that he never mentioned. Charlie, too, had never heard Ernie speak of the battle-decorated aircraft carrier. A check of the *Saratoga*'s war record shows that it was supporting the marine landings on Guadalcanal and was hit by a torpedo from a Japanese submarine a month after the Battle of Savo Island. Forced to limp back to Pearl Harbor for repairs while weathering a typhoon, *Saratoga* was very likely the ship that took Ernie back to Hawaii.

I ask Craig about *Vincennes*. Did Ernie ever mention it as they sailed Lake Ontario?

The phone line is silent as Craig ponders the question.

"I didn't know," he says after a few seconds, "he was on the *Vincennes*."

Piece by piece, Ernie's story comes together like that pile of lumber to which he's fond of referring, a shapeless pile that with some work becomes a boat or a house or a life story.

Steve Lockner, Marilyn's son, the whiskey-drinking Harley guy, tried to put together the story as well. He searched the internet for photos of *Vincennes*, thinking he might be able to get a few on the wall of the local VFW.

"They take a picture of every ship when it's being launched," he says. "I was hoping I could find one of those." Marilyn reined him in.

"Ma said, 'Don't bring that up. It gives him nightmares.'"

Perhaps it's because Steve was in the service as well, but he seemed to have gotten deeper into the story of the old sailor's last night on *Vincennes* more than most people around Ernie.

"I was called back up for Desert Storm," Steve says. "Stuck in a tent in the desert at night, all you could hear were Scud missiles coming down."

He and Ernie discussed this.

"We'd talk about how you'd listen for the shell fragments to land, so you'd know how close or how far away they were. And he'd say, yeah, he knew what I was talking about."

And then Ernie told of the nightmare sight of water on fire, all around the ship, and the decision he made that he believes saved his life.

Charlie had tried to give such scattered clues some continuity after hearing one of the old sailors at the Rochester Yacht Club describing how he'd just returned from Washington, D.C., with the Rochester chapter of Honor Flights. The national group organizes trips for the rapidly dwindling number of vets—it's estimated a thousand of them were dying every day—who wanted to see the World War II memorial in their final years.

"I thought Ernie would enjoy that," Charlie says. Indeed, "He was excited by the idea right away."

Father and son made the journey in fall 2009, after Ernie's latest round of knee surgeries had healed. The Rochester chapter, "Maybe fifty vets, each with at least one escort, plus a handful of people as guides," Charlie says, flew into D.C. for dinner, a night in a hotel, and a trip to the memorial. Veterans from throughout the country were piled into buses and driven to the site. Though their bodies sagged with age, these were men of epic stature, witnesses to events that swept across the entire planet. But the weather was miserable, the rain so heavy that the aging veterans, all likely prime candidates for pneumonia, hardly left their buses.

"Ernie was disappointed he wasn't able to get out and look for any of his old shipmates," Charlie says.

Rain or not, he'd arrived. Many never would. The World War II memorial estimates 404,800 of Ernie's fellow U.S. servicemen were killed in the war; some estimates are even higher. One section of the memorial is called the Freedom Wall, with 4,048 gold stars, each one representing one hundred Americans who died in the war.

But Ernie saw the visit to the World War II memorial as merely a social occasion, not an opportunity for more revelations. He would not find closure, that elusive concept so highly regarded by armchair analysts. Charlie and the family members who had been at that Thanksgiving dinner would have to settle for what they'd heard that day, a story they'd never dreamed existed.

* * *

Thanksgiving 2008.

"What else did you do in the war? You must have done something else."

Questioned by Charlie, urged on by family members, Ernie finally relented, describing what he could, crying through it. Then he was finished.

"Please don't ask me to talk about it again," he said afterward. "It gives me nightmares."

"The first shell hit the carpenter's shop and killed a lot of his friends," Charlie recalls Ernie telling them.

"At that time, Ernie was down below. They were all rushed up to the deck to fight fires. Everyone became a fireman. When the call came to abandon ship, they tried to put a lifejacket on him, but he refused."

One can imagine now what was going through Ernie's mind as he tried to escape the flaming warship as it slipped beneath the water, an ocean and a continent distant from the waters where he'd learned to sail and swim and dive. He was calling on the experiences of his youth. The way he'd challenge himself to swim across Canandaigua Lake. The fearlessness that comes with soaring through the air with a homemade tumbling team during high school. Wrestling with uncertainty while standing on Lock 32 before diving into the canal for the first time. Or, turning to survival instinct after falling through the ice into the canal as a young teenager, which told him he must figure out which way is up in that dark, freezing water and swim back to that hole of light or die.

That is what allowed Ernie to survive, while 332 of his shipmates did not.

"The order to abandon ship came, and they tried to put a life jacket on him," Charlie says. "The water was on fire. He didn't want to float around in the middle of that in a life jacket. He dove in and swam as far as he could underwater, maybe one hundred yards, until he came up on the other side of the fire. And that's how he survived."

TWENTY-SIX

The lake is steely gray, the sky a low ceiling of uninspiring clouds, the temperature struggling to reach fifty degrees. Soaring overhead is the new O'Rourke Bridge, named for a Rochester Civil War colonel shot dead at Gettysburg. Below, spread out along the east bank of the Genesee River, is the Genesee Yacht Club. It's a small but cozy clubhouse and a handful of metal-sided buildings, with a ten-year wait for one of the dock's fifty berths. But now they're deserted except for a few seagulls poking at something seemingly interesting near a garbage can, until they scream in disappointment and strut away.

Sailing season is over. This is the final haul-out day. The boats are being moved to the gray gravel and mud parking area, balanced on their impossibly spindly stands, bundled in bright blue tarps for the winter. Many of the club's 128 member boats are here. Only thirteen remain to be plucked from the chilly water on this late-October morning. Ernie likes to delay *Desire*'s haul-out, leaving it to be among this last group. It is his final racing strategy of the season. "The last in, the first out," he says.

The clean winds of sailing have given way to the smells and sounds of diesel engines. Masts have been taken down and laid lengthwise on the boats, which then humbly motor their way into a basin built into the bank of the river. Brown and yellow leaves and small twigs float in the basin, crowding into the corners. Just a few hundred yards upriver, the steep banks of the Genesee are still alive with a few weeks' brief burst of the leaves' colors. Then they die and fall into the water, dodging among the dead tree branches, meandering slowly downstream. In the contemplative mood cast by the season and the orderly, almost ceremonial close to sailing, the mind drifts easily to silly allegories of the River Styx and this river of sticks.

But I digress; work is yet to be done. A towering, four-wheeled lift is driven over the top of the basin, straddling the boat. Two stout straps are positioned on either end of the keel, and the boat is hauled up. The lift moves the boat away from the basin, stopping over the spot where a forklift or a tractor has set the boat's cradle. More than a few of the owners refer to their boats as "Baby." After the hull is power washed, the boat is set down on its cradle and towed away, and the haul-out crew moves on to the next boat.

The operation is well practiced.

"A lot of these guys are retired; they're not working anymore; they spend all week on the haul-out," says one of the club members, Gerard Fisher. His boat, *Bebob*, has just come out of the water and now he's helping with the next, *Kraken*.

"Last year the average age of the members was sixty-two," Fisher says. "This year it's sixty-three. They're getting new members. But most of them are old." Fisher has about a decade to go before he reaches that average.

At ninety-three, Ernie skews the numbers a bit. He has a green plastic chair at the edge of the activity, but he's not using it much. Instead, he scuttles around with his crab-like walk along the edge of the basin, holding a line or using a boat hook to keep a boat from bumping against the concrete sides. He's not trying to run the show, just staying involved.

"He's a great guy," Fisher says. "A lot of these old-timers, you put twenty of them in a room and you get twenty different opinions on something. If Ernie walks in the room, you still have twenty opinions. He doesn't say anything unless he thinks you're really screwing up."

Ernie's not saying much this morning. He's too busy conducting reconnaissance. He points to *Kraken*.

"He's the same rating as me," he says as *Kraken* hangs in the air. "That'll be my competition next year."

The boats look helpless in the hoist, their privates exposed. Rudders and propellers at the back. Midway up, the keel. A few smaller boats, like *Bebob*, have centerboard keels that crank up inside the boat, like what Ernie used to install on his Snipes. But most have heavy fixed keels protruding three or four feet from the bottom of the boat, squares of cast iron with a tapered leading edge yet blunt like a wood maul. These counterbalance the weight of the mast and provide enough resistance to keep the boat from sliding sideways in the wind.

Many of the experienced club members are grumbling that today's haul-out is going slower than usual. *Freedom*'s mast rolls off the side of the boat and into the basin and must be fetched by a crane. Some of the boats aren't quite ready, and the minor delays add up.

Ernie's daughter Jan is also here. *Desire* is out of the water now, and she runs the palm of her hand along the fiberglass hull where the power washing has left the area below the waterline a dull blue-gray.

"I missed a spot there," she says, pointing to a smudge that looks minor.

"You miss that mud or grease, it can be a pain in the ass to get off in the spring."

She pushes on some tiny blisters beneath the paint on the cast-iron keel until they pop and bleed water. These imperfections are the size of a ladybug. They will be sanded smooth and the bottom painted after winter recedes.

Ernie doesn't regard the haul-out as an end. The seasons are as much a part of sailing as they are to farming. Planning, preparation, anticipation, a fresh start each spring. "You've got something to look forward to," he says. "I know guys who move to Florida, they put their boats in the water, they hardly use them. I know one guy, he told me he would go out once a week, then once a month. Now it's about once a season."

* * *

Florida. God's waiting room. They probably pipe Vangelis through the speakers there, as well, but it sounds more thrilling when you're riding a five-masted clipper ship into the sunset. Ernie says his brother Frank, ninety-eight years old at the time, was complaining he could only hit a golf ball two hundred yards when he reached age ninety-five. Golfing at age ninety-five. Two hundred yards. Well, maybe it just looks like two hundred yards when your eyes grow old. But Frank worked for every day he got, just like Ernie.

You've also got to be lucky for admission to the Century Club, even if you have to finish the last stretch with a walker. As he talks about his brother retired in Florida, Ernie begins thinking about Tampa Bay, a body of water that he has sailed.

"I wasn't impressed," he says. "Even the wind didn't feel right. You've got to watch for buoys; there's a lot of shallow spots. Here, you just go out and go wherever you want."

Frank's fifth-floor apartment was in Bradenton, just south of Tampa Bay. Ernie recalls watching from there as a planned detonation took down some of the remains of an overland section of the old Sunshine Skyway Bridge. Ernie starts telling a story he read about a guy who was standing on the deck of a 580-foot bulk freighter back in 1980 as it was trying to pass under the Sunshine Skyway in a near-zero-visibility rainstorm. *Summit Venture* crashed into the bridge, and a center section of it buckled and collapsed into the bay. Some of it came down onto the ship as well, where a section with a hatch for maintaining the bridge was fortuitously left unsecured, the opening landing right over a guy standing on the deck. Pure luck.

"The guy wasn't even scratched," Ernie says. "A bus landed on its top and everybody was crushed. That was it. Cars went in, they managed to crawl out. So you can't worry about those things."

Perhaps it's simply one of those oft-repeated urban legends. A section of the bridge did land on *Summit Venture*, but looking back at the news reports, no guy on the deck caught a lucky break that morning. Maybe that was another ship, another bridge. A bus did plunge into the water, and twenty-six people in it died. Six cars fell off the bridge, and all nine people in them died. But the driver of a pickup truck that went off the bridge caught a different lucky break. The truck hit *Summit Venture* first, breaking its fall, before it slid into the bay. The guy swam to the surface, the only survivor among those who fell into the water. The fact that he had lived and the others died haunted him for the rest of his life.

An act of God. That's what the coast guard and a state grand jury ruled the disaster. Casualty report aside, Ernie's recollection of the bridge disaster was close. Perhaps it's not surprising that he'd take an interest in such an incident. Fragile human bodies generally lose in calamitous events involving massive amounts of iron and steel and deep water. Narrow escapes from death that certainly matched this one, as the Sunshine Skyway fell into the water: a Buick with four men in it skidded to a stop, the left front wheel fourteen inches from where the span had broken off 150 feet above the water.

In reading about the bridge disaster, it's striking how some of the details feel like what might have happened on *Vincennes* on the night that it sank. I allowed myself to imagine what it must have been: Ernie down below, the thunderous noise, the loudspeaker, tinny like a crystal radio's punch-by-punch portrait of the Dempsey-Tunney fight, announcing "bombs falling . . . coming toward us." The steel of the huge ship shuddering as the shells and torpedoes hit, the black smoke, the darkness when the lights go out. Men moving in an orderly fashion as they've been trained, feeling their way through darkness. The air roaring and whistling from below as it's displaced by the water pushing its way into the ship, the clatter of machinery and coffee cups hitting the floor, the floor turning over, the search for the way out through familiar corridors increasingly rendered unfamiliar. The death groan of the ship as it feels itself breaking. There's the hatch! Shouts of "it's every man for himself," "help pick up the man who's stumbled in front of you," "move on, he's dead," into the fire, fire, fire. The pumps aren't working, nothing is working, the training is irrelevant. The ship shudders as it is struck again by another torpedo, and the dark water rushes toward the deck at an insane angle. This is it, this is it. The understanding that men and ship soon will be overwhelmed by water. Men shouting, shouting, "abandon ship." What about the men in the engine rooms? Never mind they'll never make it this far. Men crushed beneath broken steel and burned to death at their posts, the ship settling like a dying prehistoric beast. There's the water. It's happening so fast there's no time to think. Men carrying a life raft, here's a lifejacket, stepping over body parts, slipping on blood, to the railing, the dark water on fire, the sea, and the only chance to save yourself. . . .

* * *

In the days following the collapse of the Sunshine Skyway, a diver descended some sixty feet to the floor of the bay, drifting through the bridge wreckage and lost cars, and noted that the noise from the collision and from the bridge falling into the water seemed to have scared off much of the marine life. Ernie himself remarked on such a phenomenon while based in Maui. There were no whales to be seen in those whale-watching waters in the months, more than a year even, after the attack on Pearl Harbor some 111 miles away.

Maybe that is also what saved many of the men floating that early morning in Iron Bottom Sound, in a wartime irony. The explosions that tore apart their ships might have bought the sailors some time in the generally shark-heavy waters.

Perhaps fate, like a surly-looking hitchhiker, is best left in the rear-view mirror, unexamined. Ships sink, spouses die, kids fall through the canal ice and only some of them fight their way back to the surface. Most often, the outcome of these events is out of our control. Outliving everyone around you isn't actually a question of mortality.

Outliving everyone means, Ernie says, "how you feel when your time is up."

If he were still climbing that Mayan pyramid, one step for each day, after ninety-three years Ernie would have ascended 4,200 steps. Plus another twenty-three for leap years. Quite a journey.

"I saw radio," he says.

"Television. Jet planes, just to name a few. Super railways. We had railways when I was a kid, but not super railways. And the computer."

* * *

The haul-out is finished. *Desire* is positioned right where Ernie wants it. At the front of the line, bow facing the basin, pointing toward next spring. His final racing strategy. Last one in, first one out.

TWENTY-SEVEN

About three weeks before Christmas 2012, I was sitting with Ernie in his kitchen. He pulled the oxygen mask away from his face, took a sip of merlot, and told me he didn't expect to live much longer.

I wasn't convinced. He'd already survived a handful of episodes that would have been the end of lesser men, including a major heart attack a couple of weeks earlier that had indeed killed him until the EMTs who rushed him to Rochester General Hospital beat on his chest, prodding his heart back into action. And he'd survived the worst defeat ever inflicted on the U.S. Navy, the Battle of Savo Island. Ernie knew a lot about a lot of things, but one thing I didn't think this guy knew much about was dying.

He'd had another health scare that year. Pneumonia. Dangerous territory for a ninety-five-year-old man. He made it through, but his family and I decided we'd better get on with self-publishing *Chasing the Wind*.

The whole point of the last year and a half had been to pull together this life story in a way that the old man could hold in those carpentry-battered hands of his. I sifted through family photos, bought an aerial shot of *Vincennes* from the National Archives, shopped for a self-publishing company, and attended a writers' conference where one speaker advised us that the average self-published book sold forty-eight copies.

Forty-eight copies. I reminded myself that *Chasing the Wind* was about Ernie, not my ego. By May I'd pulled it all together, with the first two hundred copies delivered to Ernie and Marilyn's door just a week before the Sunday afternoon book release party I'd arranged at Java's at the Market, a coffee shop in the Rochester Public Market.

In three hours, I watched as 150, maybe 200 people—I don't know the exact number—grazed over the vast spread of food prepared that morning by Margaret. Caprese salad on a stick, tortellini, cheeses, olives, pineapple and ham skewers, sangria, and the salmon I'd smoked the day before. Ernie and I signed copy after copy after copy of *Chasing the Wind*. About ninety in all.

My friend Kinloch Nelson played guitar, Patrick Flanigan read a letter from the mayor about Ernie, and people applauded. I read an excerpt from the book and people laughed and cheered. People took photos and they cheered Ernie, who'd made it this far. And they congratulated me, even though all I'd done was what I've been doing for years. Write.

I went home that evening, some of the neighbors came over, and I sat on the deck, a fire flickering in the chiminea, and drank wine until I couldn't keep my eyes open any longer.

* * *

I was on Amazon.com a couple of weeks later, fascinated with the idea that I could type my name—Jeff Spevak—into the search engine and have a book with my name on it pop up. I had to search for my name specifically, having had no idea that the title *Chasing the Wind* was so popular among romance novelists, spiritual gurus, and environmentalists (*Chasing the Wind: Regulating Air Pollution in the Common Law State*). I clicked on my book, scrolled down, and . . . *Wow! Someone reviewed my book!*—and gave it four out of five stars! The last paragraph of the review:

> I've known Jeff Spevak since we were assigned seats, alphabetically, next to each other in homeroom in junior high and have been reading his work since. Over the years Spevak has developed a keen eye for looking at ordinary situations and ordinary people and writing a story worth telling—and reading.

I wouldn't be surprised if the first reviews of most unknown writers come from people with whom they drank a hell of a lot of beer. Mike, who wrote the review, probably won't remember this, but I distinctly recall sitting in a booth in a dark Kent State bar called Ray's Pub more than thirty years ago telling him that my dream was someday to be one of those writers whose name on the book cover is bigger than the title.

That summer of 2012 would also mark the seventieth anniversary of the Battle of Savo Island. I emailed some of the major news organizations—NPR, the *New York Times*—serious outlets that I imagined might be interested in the anniversary and in the story of a veteran who had been a part of it and was featured in a new book that I just happened to write. I heard back from no one. As the anniversary of the battle neared, I heard and read nothing of it. The country reminisces on Pearl Harbor and the Battle of the Bulge each year. Defeats that, through resilience of character, ultimately led to triumph. Yet we find no time or space for Savo Island, perhaps because we have no taste for such a resounding defeat overshadowed by the giant Battle of Midway two months earlier, in which the United States sunk four Japanese aircraft carriers in one day.

You've likely seen that story told in grainy newsreel footage hundreds of times on the History Channel. Midway was the turning point in the war, the historians like to say. It's inconvenient to the easy narrative when that road dips and swings one direction, then the other. Savo Island, even as a subtext of the ultimately successful Battle of Guadalcanal, is comfortably forgotten. Even though the men who fought there were equally resilient, equally brave as the men who died at Pearl Harbor and the Battle of the Bulge.

Yet it's also in our nature to revisit tragedy. Microsoft cofounder Paul Allen had the resources to do so. He led expeditions that found a handful of iconic war sinkings, including the aircraft carrier *Lexington*, lost in the Battle of Coral Sea, and the cruiser *Indianapolis*, sunk by a Japanese submarine in the final days of World War II as it was returning from a mission delivering components for the atomic bomb dropped on Hiroshima. Robert Ballard's 1992 exploration of the Savo Island wrecks had discovered *Quincy* and *Canberra*, *Vincennes* and *Astoria* remaining lost in the dark fathoms. Allen's group arrived in 2015 armed with the latest in underwater survey technology, including side-scan sonar and remotely operated vehicles. They found twenty-nine of the estimated fifty wrecks on the floor of Iron Bottom Sound. That included all four of the rusting, ripped-up cruisers sunk in the Battle of Savo Island. Among the startling images of this silent ghost fleet: a gaping, almost perfectly round hole from an eight-inch shell that nearly dots the "I" where the name *Vincennes* would have been on the ship's stern.

Because *Chasing the Wind* was self-published and I had designed the cover, I could have fulfilled the dream I told my friend Mike about that night three decades ago in Ray's Pub and made my name as big as I wanted on the front of the book. I didn't. Ernie's story dwarfs guys like me.

I thought I'd be done with *Chasing the Wind* after the release party. Not so. One of the local morning TV talk shows invited me to chat about the book, as did a DJ friend on one of the morning noncommercial radio shows. People were calling me about doing promotional events. A handful of book clubs, almost always women, including a Mormon book club. I did readings and signings at the local literary center, small book festivals, assisted-living facilities, the yacht clubs, churches, gift shops, even at a couple of folk music concerts. Some of the excellent independent bookstores in town carried *Chasing the Wind*. My goal had been to sell a thousand copies of the book, and after nine months we made it—and beyond, selling twelve hundred copies.

It was all small stuff, a dozen books sold here, six there. Aside from Amazon.com, I'd been frustrated by attempts to place it in big outlets. Wegmans, the huge regional grocery chain that bragged about selling apples grown by local farmers, told me I'd have to go through its corporate office, a paperwork-heavy process that would take months. A buyer for Barnes & Noble informed me that self-published books "are for friends and relatives."

Ernie usually accompanied me to the literary events but not always. When he was there, I'd read from the chapter on the overnight Freedom Cup race, the one where the rest of *Desire*'s crew slept as Ernie sailed for home, watching the sun rise. If Ernie wasn't there, I'd read an excerpt from the war. Ernie was proud of the book, but he never read the chapters about Savo Island. When someone at a signing asked him about the war, Ernie would shake his head no, point, and say, "It's in the book."

Chasing the Wind seemed to give him a new purpose in life, but it was temporary. Even if I wouldn't allow myself to admit it, Ernie was fading, relying on a walker to get around and then, after the heart attack, oxygen. I visited him at the hospital as he recovered. He looked great and described the whole process to me from falling ill at his house, the ride to the hospital, how the EMTs worked over him when he went into cardiac arrest in the hospital lobby, and the specifics of the surgical procedure.

As we talked, an odd woman was scurrying around the room, taking care of little details, as a nurse might, except she wasn't wearing the uniform. It was Pat. She'd flown in from Arizona after hearing what had happened.

One of the last signings was in November 2012 at Herrema's Market Place, a local independent grocery just a few blocks from Ernie's house. Maybe it was because Ernie was a neighborhood guy, maybe because the store put it on a rack alongside *The National Enquirer*, but Herrema's sold hundreds of copies. I didn't expect to see Ernie that day as I was setting up the little table and our pile of books. But then, there he came through the front door in his wheeled walker, dragging along a bottle of oxygen, still mad because the doctors forbade him from driving after the heart attack.

* * *

When Ernie told me he didn't expect to live much longer—adding that he was OK with that—he had the facts on his side. The wheeled walker, the bottle of oxygen. And he proved to be right once again. Rushed to the hospital with his heart giving out and his wife Marilyn begging him to not leave her on Christmas Day, Ernie badgered the nurses throughout the evening—"Is it still Christmas? Is it still Christmas?"—until it was safely past midnight and Marilyn had gone home. Only then did Ernie finally let go at about 1:45 in the morning.

Julie called my house the next morning. Margaret took the message and told me when I got home from the office. I just nodded and walked away. It was over.

A strange reaction perhaps. I'd seen similar reactions before. Years ago, I'd been visiting my parents at their winter home in Florida. One of those vast tracts of red-tiled, single-floor homes lining gently curving streets. One evening Margaret and I were walking through the neighborhood when we came to a house with a couple of emergency vehicles parked in front of it. I recognized the house. An elderly couple, distant relatives of my father, lived there. From the way the firemen and EMT personnel were behaving—just standing around in the driveway, no sense of urgency—it did not look good. We hustled home and I told my dad, "I think something bad's happening at your cousin's house."

"Oh no!" he bellowed. "I'm not getting involved in that!"

My dad's father had died when he was about ten years old. All through his life, that's how I saw him deal with life's big things, like death: by walking away. Maybe I wasn't as bad; I'd seen enough of how other people behave. But I was also wired the same way.

The night after Ernie died, the first big storm of the winter hit Rochester. I lay awake in bed most of the night listening to the wind fling itself against the side of the house, thinking about what Ernie had been through at Savo Island. I thought about a phone call that Marilyn had gotten from an old marine who'd been on Guadalcanal. He told her they could see the battle raging around Savo Island that night, and they saw the U.S. and Australian ships burning. They felt helpless, unable to do anything for those guys dying out there that night.

"He made it past Christmas," Julie told me a couple of days later.

She and Marilyn had just read Ernie's online obituary in the newspaper.

"We were laughing because it was the shortest one there," Julie said. "And yet he did so much in his life."

* * *

Hundreds of people showed up for the wake at the Genesee Yacht Club. Ernie was cremated, as he'd asked. His family and his fellow sailors delayed his final wish until summer, when the weather was better and everyone had the opportunity to get their boats back on the lake. About twenty boats sailed out into Lake Ontario with Ernie aboard *Desire* for one last voyage. There, he was scattered to the water.

"Powder off the side of the boat," as Ernie had said.

Long afterward, I encountered people who wanted to talk about Ernie. A friend showed me a photo of a grave marker he'd spotted in Mount Adnah Cemetery in Fulton, New York, about an hour-and-a-half drive east of Rochester. The marker was for a sailor named Russell Almon Rogers, the stone identifying him as a fire controlman on *Vincennes*; Rogers would have manned the ship's range-finding gear.

The inscription read, "Lost at Sea off Savo Island, Aug. 10, 1942." There was no body beneath that stone lying among family members, just a remembrance. I wondered if Ernie had known the man. If he knew a shipmate had once lived so close.

So many people had stories about Ernie. Or meaningful anecdotes. Here's my final, most treasured image of the old man: Near the end of that final sailing season, I'd head over to the Genesee Yacht Club where Ernie kept his boat. His wheeled walker sat at the edge of the empty dock. Ernie and *Desire* were gone, out somewhere on the lake.

* * *

There would be one more public reading of *Chasing the Wind*. I'd booked it before Ernie died as part of the library's "Rochester's Rich History Series: How We Became Who We Are." The reading was to be in the older of the two downtown library buildings, the cooler Rundel Memorial Building. Supposedly haunted, its marble facade chiseled with old inscriptions like, "The shadows will be behind you if you walk into the light."

Libraries are a foundation of our communities, far more meaningful than football stadiums or the air show that takes over the nearby airport every year. I used our library a lot when I was a kid growing up in a suburb of Cleveland. When I was working in downtown Rochester, I'd walk the couple of blocks from the office, hand the homeless guy a dollar, cross the Broad Street Bridge over the Genesee River, and duck into ours for forty-five minutes or an hour. I usually check out ten CDs, the limit, and one or two books.

A few weeks before that final reading, I had forgotten the exact date and called up the library website. I couldn't find a reference to the Rochester's Rich History Series right away, so I searched for *Chasing the Wind*. Instead of the talk, up came a listing for copies of *Chasing the Wind* carried in the Monroe County Library System. I hadn't even known this: Thirteen copies of the book were listed. Two at the central library and one at each of eleven branch libraries around the surrounding suburbs and towns and villages.

More than half of them were checked out. It took my breath away.

What would Ernie have made of that?

* * *

The reading was on a snowy, bitterly cold Sunday afternoon. I was stunned that eighteen people actually bothered to show up. I started by reading the section on the Freedom Cup race. Then I moved on to the war. The part that ends with the quote from *The Winds of War*: "In a world so rich and lovely, could his children find nothing better to do than to dig iron from the ground and work it into vast grotesque engines for blowing each other up?"

And as I started talking a little more about Ernie—this would be my last chance, and I had something to say—I started to get choked up, stumbling over the words. Someone handed me a tissue. I recovered, backed up, talked a little more, then returned to the words that had gotten to me. I knew it was trouble, that I wouldn't make it through them this second time, either, and I didn't. But I wanted to say this:

"He was a great guy."

* * *

Few of us are allowed the privilege of witnessing a century of life's rich, and inevitably painful, pageant. Ernie Coleman nearly made it.

He was a relatively common fellow, as carpenters tend to be. Nevertheless, friends and family saw him as heroic in ways difficult to define. Perhaps it was his old-school, hands-on work ethic, a quality we've witnessed in many people who grew up in the hardship of the Great Depression. Perhaps it was his success as a sailor, winning races for decades on Lake Ontario. But other sailors win races. Perhaps it was how he stepped in as the head of a household full of kids blossoming into teenagers and quelled the rebellion. But we've already seen *The Brady Bunch.* Perhaps it was his plainspoken manner or the twinkling devil on his shoulder that said yes to a scotch on the rocks even as he was closing in on ninety-six.

Perhaps it's because Ernie lived so damn long. In his final years he was instructed by his doctors to take it easy, but it's against the law to tie the guy to a chair. When I stopped by his house one Saturday afternoon in 2010, I saw a ninety-four-year-old man out back, painting the prefabricated toolshed that his family had just purchased for him. When he finished, he sat down in the kitchen and had a glass of red wine.

His family rented a hall for his ninety-fifth birthday party and had to cut off the guest list at about two hundred—this despite the fact that Ernie had outlived many of his friends.

Ernie was a common hero, but also a war hero; the few details he made available known to a few family members and friends. Certainly no one ever knew the whole story. He was a witness to an epic moment in history that he didn't talk about. He filed it away in the place where we hide pain so that we can move on with our lives. He never thought of himself as a hero in this larger way, although readers will likely disagree.

The world's armed forces fill its sophisticated warships and tanks with farm boys, high school football stars, class valedictorians, vocational school welding students, dropouts, HVAC apprentices, store clerks, and kids from the city who never thought about going any farther than the transit bus system will take them, as well as young men who killed silver foxes for rich women's fashions. And they expect these kids to go out and win wars. Ernie and his shipmates did the best that they could in those uncertain circumstances. A handful of chapters in this book confront that moment and scattered references are elsewhere. Ernie preferred not to acknowledge them, and he had the right to make that choice. Few of us have ever had to face the horror that he faced. The human psyche is far more fragile than we care to admit.

Most of us hope to live meaningful lives and have an impact on those closest to us. We probably won't change the course of world events. Yet the stories of people like Ernie are useful in that larger way, because they are the truth. If those truths give us pause before we rush men and women into harm's way, that's good. If those truths simply show a young sailor how to find an elusive breeze on an otherwise peaceful lake, that's good as well.

INDEX